by John Sedgwick

Illustrations by Terry Allen

NIGHT VISION

Confessions of Gil Lewis, Private Eye

SIMON AND SCHUSTER
NEW YORK

SIMON AND SCHUSTER and colophon are trademarks of Simon & Schuster
Designed by Irving Perkins Associates
Manufactured in the United States of America
10 9 8 7 6 5 4 3 2 1

Library of Congress Cataloging in Publication Data

Sedgwick, John, [date].
    Night vision.

    1. Detectives—Massachusetts—Boston.   I. Lewis, Gil.   I. Title.
HV7914.S36   1982   363.2′89′0924   [B]   82-10290

ISBN 0-671-43237-0

AUTHOR'S NOTE

The stories told in this book are true. Except for such well-known figures as Howard Hughes and Joseph P. Kennedy III, I have changed the names and some identifying details of the characters to protect the individuals' privacy. Gil Lewis does indeed exist, and can be reached under that name at his agency in Wollaston, Massachusetts. Portions of this book originally appeared as "The Lewis Files" in *The Real Paper,* published in Cambridge, MA.

                                                                J.S.

For Megan —

CONTENTS

PREFACE

I first met Gil Lewis at a small Greek restaurant in Cambridge, Massachusetts. The editor of an alternative weekly newspaper was considering me for the job of writing a column about Lewis' exploits, but the deal hinged on my getting along with the detective at lunch. I was apprehensive about it since, like most people, I assumed all private eyes were shady, somewhat dangerous types in trench coats, given to hard drinking and low humor.

Lewis was waiting in the restaurant lobby when I arrived. (I would learn later that the private investigator always comes early.) He was dressed in his customary brown leather jacket and blue jeans and, far from being the hulking tough guy I expected, he approached me almost shyly. As we sat down for lunch and started talking I was impressed by his warmth and intelligence. It did not take long to recognize that he had a far-ranging curiosity, a lively sense of humor, and a wonderful way of expressing himself. And the stories he had to tell . . .

In short, we hit it off, and the series was launched. When it ran its course after twenty-six installments, Gil and I were still eager for more. That's when we turned our attention to this book.

In doing the research I met regularly with Gil for breakfast at his favorite hangout, the Mug 'n' Muffin near his home in Wollaston. We usually went back to his house for coffee afterward to discuss his cases in more detail. And we spoke often over the phone. I rode with him on some of his nightly surveillances, too, although I had a tendency to nod off around midnight, long before Lewis' work was done.

As a journalist, I have interviewed a wide range of people from oceanographers to pool sharks, but none have been so patient or

11

helpful as Gil. Even as I waded through yet another list of questions that to him must often have seemed very much beside the point, Lewis would just take another puff on his ever-present Muriel Coronella, think for a moment, and give me the straight answers.

I checked all his stories—interviewing clients, examining records, reading newspaper accounts, talking to cops who had worked the case from the other side—but I never once caught Lewis out. He stuck to the facts as closely as if he had been on the witness stand before a judge and jury. He had his own files to rely on, but his memory was so extraordinarily acute he rarely had to refer to them. Even cases that had taken place fifteen or twenty years ago he could recall in full, vivid detail. It has been a pleasure to work with him.

Of all the people who helped and encouraged me, I'd like to give special thanks to R. D. Rosen, Pamela Painter, Marie Cantlon, and Pepe Karmel. Julie Eberhart and Leah Osterman were unstinting in their help with the typing. John Brockman has been a marvelous agent. And my editor, Fred Hills, and his assistant, Martha Cochrane, have shown the sort of patient guidance with a first-time author that I'll always be grateful for. It's been a long journey for Gil and me, traveling from "The Lewis Files" in *The Real Paper* to the present volume, but it's been a great trip. Finally, I'd like to thank my wife, the writer Megan Marshall, without whose help, support, and love this book would never have been written.

"People are always telling me I look tired. Well, I'm not. I've been this way ever since I was a kid."

ONE

To Hell with Sam Spade

It's midnight and the clapboard houses lining the narrow street are quiet, the doors bolted and shades pulled. A dog is barking somewhere, a few teen-agers are still straggling home from their dates, and cars are rushing along an adjoining avenue. Otherwise, the whole place might be asleep.

Yet in the row of parked cars by the curb, their chrome bumpers and shiny sides gleaming under the streetlamps, a man sits silently at the wheel. He seems to be sleeping, for he's slumped down deep in his seat, motionless, a baseball cap pulled down low over his eyes. He's hard to see because the windows are so heavily tinted—specially designed, like so much in this man's life, to keep out inquiring glances. And he's parked away from the light.

He is not sleeping. A cigar, clenched between his teeth, sends up a slender trail of smoke. Gil Lewis is not even resting. He's watching, his dark eyes fixed on a second-story bedroom window three houses down.

There, the private investigator believes, his client's husband is carrying on an affair with a divorcée. Lewis has tracked the man to this shadowy side street three times this month, and when he showed again, parking out front and running up the front steps,

Lewis knew the end of this case was in sight. Although the bedroom shade is drawn, the lights are on behind it, the only ones still burning in the house. Lewis is waiting for the couple to turn off the lights—legal proof the two are committing adultery. After three hours, Lewis has smoked two packets of Muriel Coronellas. He'll probably go through a few packets more before he's finished for the night. But that's fine with Lewis. He's content to wait.

"I suppose my life is a little eerie," he admits. "I'm a shadow, an invisible man drifting through other people's lives." Certainly the husband now dallying on the second floor knows nothing of him, and he probably never will. When the divorce proceedings begin and the man's attorney hears that Gil Lewis has been on the case, he'll probably suggest to his client that he settle without a trial. That saves the man the embarrassment of hearing Lewis recite all the grim details of the infidelity in open court. So Lewis may never appear, but his presence will be felt. His report, typically ten pages, with the most incriminating material held back lest it fall into a blackmailer's hands, could cost the husband his house, half his earnings, and the right to see his children except on alternate weekends. Yet the detective makes no apologies. "I'm just a reporter," he insists. "I don't make up the story. I just write it down."

At forty-eight, Lewis has been in the detective business for more than twenty years. A shade under five-eleven, with a calm, open face and gray hair, Lewis could be any one of the thousands of Irish Catholic businessmen jamming the Boston streets at rush hour. And that's just the way the investigator wants it. He used to wear a mustache, but shaved it off one morning on impulse when he decided he was wasting too much time on it. "I even *waxed* the fucking thing," he says. "Can you imagine?" He still wears oversized rimless glasses to hide the bags that droop slightly below his gentle brown eyes—under the weight, one imagines, of everything he's seen. "People are always telling me I look tired," he says. "Well, I'm *not*. I've been this way ever since I was a kid."

Lewis can blend into just about any crowd. He could pass for his brother Leon, an English professor at the University of Wisconsin, or for his other brother, Wilfred, a truck driver in nearby Brockton, just as easily. He can adapt his conversational style to any situation, too. "I can shut the polysyllables off or turn them up, depending on who I'm talking to," he says. "I swear a lot, but that's just the job. People expect a private investigator to use street language because the street is where I spend my time."

Only his strength singles him out. "I may have an eighty-year-old face," Lewis likes to say, "but I've got a twenty-year-old body." Although he believes he inherited his frame from his father, a career patrolman, Lewis beefed himself up early for a boxing career that never materialized and has kept in shape ever since with a two-hour weight-lifting session every morning before breakfast. He still looks as though he could go fifteen rounds if necessary. On the job, an impressive physique can come in handy when he has to emerge from the shadows to question a murderer or collect evidence from those who aren't inclined to give it. He habitually stands with his legs spread and his hands on his hips to make the most of his imposing appearance.

When Lewis was just starting out he used to pack himself into a business suit every day, but now that he feels more secure in his profession he's opted for blue jeans, an open shirt, and, in chilly weather, a leather jacket. The casual dress works as a disguise as well, since, as he says, "everybody expects the trench coat and the fedora." But more than that, Lewis simply feels comfortable in such clothes, and that's important for those long nights behind the wheel with only a Muriel Coronella for company.

Because of the Hollywood associations of the term "private eye," Lewis calls himself a "professional investigator," or simply "an investigator." Unlike most detectives, Lewis sticks exclusively to what he calls "pure investigation"—that means no security work in department stores or bodyguarding VIPs. "I don't want to have to open doors for people," he says.

"Domestic cases, criminal investigations, and missing-persons work are the big three in my business," he goes on. "Domestic" is a code word for the messy, bitterly fought, sometimes even bloody divorce cases in which matrimonial lawyers hire Lewis to shadow the other party for a month or two to see if he or she has picked up another lover on the sly. In puritan Massachusetts, at least, such indiscretions still raise the ante on any settlement. Domestic work holds few thrills for the detective, but the money's good, often pulling in his preferred rate of $500 a day, plus expenses.

On many of his criminal investigations, by contrast, Lewis is lucky if he breaks even, for he can't bring himself to refuse indigent clients who have nowhere else to turn. Lewis has worked on countless murders, assaults, robberies, criminal fraud cases, allegations of police brutality, and more sex crimes than he'd care to name. One of his clients was "hitchhike murderer" Anthony Jackson, a man credited by the FBI with more than twenty killings, a state record. The crime may vary, but Lewis' task is always the same— to uncover evidence and dig up witnesses to, as he says, "put the pieces back together." It's up to the defense attorney to argue the client's innocence; Lewis just unearths the facts.

It's with missing-persons cases that Lewis works magic. He's turned up nearly two hundred vanished husbands, runaway children, missing heirs, and simply old friends who have drifted out of touch, some of them gone as long as half a century. He even located an elderly man for whom a dowager had developed a passion during a forty-five-minute trip on a commuter train. And, in a memorable sequence, the *National Enquirer* once hired him to find the girlfriend of Joseph P. Kennedy III and then to locate Howard Hughes. Lewis has developed the right contacts and refined his techniques to the point where he can produce many of the missing in two weeks.

In his jack-of-all-trades occupation, Lewis has also run background checks for employers suspicious of their employees, and for parents worried about a prospective in-law. He has traced abducted children and recovered stolen property. He has done some undercover industrial espionage and assisted the victims of death threats, as well.

"A detective is like a gold miner," says Lewis. "You have to sift a lot of dirt for specks of the truth, and sometimes you'll get sidetracked on something that turns out to have no value, but you have to examine it carefully all the same. Eventually, when you find that lump of gold, you own it. You have come up with the answer and you have cold, hard facts to support it. And you have done that on your own, because you had the patience to get out there in the hundred-degree heat and dig.

"You hear a lot about the wisecracking private eye," he continues, "but that's a load of crap. When people come to me they're

really down. There's nothing funny about them. These people are *victims*." Among his clients were the seventeen-year-old in search of the father who skipped out when she was three; the unemployed black father of two charged with a murder he swears he didn't commit; the blind newlywed gang-raped in her backyard; and the middle-aged woman who fears she's going insane because her philandering husband has lied to her so convincingly about his nightly whereabouts.

"And I don't take time off, either," Lewis says. "If I ever thought I could have saved somebody if I hadn't gone to that movie or taken that walk, I couldn't live with myself. In every case I'm dealing with somebody's life. The clients always come first." In twenty years he has taken but one vacation and that for only seven days. He works past midnight practically every night of the week. He rarely observes weekends or holidays, since those are the best times to catch his subjects at play. He spent last Thanksgiving watching an overweight businessman and his girlfriend devour a large turkey.

Realizing that perhaps his mind was too much on his cases, Lewis once decided he would learn how to relax and bought himself seven books on self-hypnosis. He mastered the technique in a day and a half, hypnotizing himself and his secretary. He did have some trouble, though, because one of the preliminary steps involved thinking back to a time when he had been fully relaxed in the past. Lewis couldn't think of any.

"Driving," he says, "that's my therapy." For a real blowout, he'll take off on his motorcycle, a chrome-laden BMW 1000, to zoom down a country road at a hundred miles an hour. "The bike's great," he says, "because you've got to concentrate so hard on staying alive, all the shit in your head just washes right out."

Seeing himself as a combination therapist and problem-solver, Lewis doesn't think much about the supposed hazards of the trade. He owns a small Remington seven-shot automatic and an "over-under" Derringer he was given by a grateful client, but he's never fired either one and rarely carries them. Most of the time he wears an empty gun holster on his belt. Since he's the only one to know it's empty, he figures that's deterrent enough.

But he was shot at once on a ghetto tenement stairway when he was mistaken for a burglar. The bullet grazed his leather jacket, but missed him. Another time he was knifed by a mugger in a housing project. "I felt a wetness," he recalls tersely, "so I went down to City Hospital to get stitched up. But in general the dangers I face are nothing compared with the guy who runs your average grocery store in a bad neighborhood. Those guys get their heads blown off for a pound of baloney."

And Lewis isn't impressed by the fancy gadgetry of his trade, either. The only camera he owns is a Kodak Instamatic, the kind that costs about $25 and fits in a shirt pocket; he gets the prints developed at a corner Fotomat. "None of my cars are special, either," he says. "If I fell in love with one of them and it broke down, I'd be out of action for a couple of days worrying." He was once given a miniature tape recorder as a present from a client, but he never uses the machine or any other on interviews, feeling it will make the witness self-conscious. For the same reason he rarely even takes notes. He listens for hours, then writes everything down from memory later.

And, while he is familiar with electronic stress analyzers, Lewis has his own methods for telling when someone is lying. Some of the local police have taken to calling him The Human Polygraph; he once matched their machine point for point on a lie-detector test. They were testing a businessman accused of torching a house to incinerate a former partner as he slept. While the machine probed the suspect's galvanic skin response, Lewis could tell by the way the man's jaw tightened and fingers went stiff every time he was trying to con them. "Everybody freezes up when they tell a lie," says Lewis. "They always force it."

———

To qualify for a license in Massachusetts, investigators have to pay a $750 fee, post a $5,000 bond, submit three references, and have three years' experience in law enforcement. Most other states, by contrast, leave the matter up to the local police chief, and that can lead to much laxer standards. The state of Oregon, for instance, not long ago licensed a twelve-year-old.

Nevertheless, for all the private investigators lurking just around the corner on television detective shows, exceedingly few exist in real life. Of the 220 licenses issued last year in Massachusetts, Lewis believes that no more than three went to genuine private investigators, operating as he does, with no other source of income.

"There isn't enough money in it," Lewis says. "There may have been once, but not anymore. Now most investigators have been swallowed up by the big security firms. Lots of guys call themselves private investigators, but they're really just ten-bucks-an-hour security guards who get thrown an investigative case by the boss twice a year. And the ones who do go it alone with their own investigative agency usually have another job to pay the bills, or they're living off a pension. That's why so many private investigators are ex-FBI guys, and retired cops. They need that $750-a-month pension money to survive.

"And it's a tough business in other ways too," Lewis goes on. "There's no formal training to tell you how to do the job. You've got to figure it out as you go along. I've probably learned more about interviewing a witness from watching Johnny Carson talk to people than anything else. There are correspondence courses you can take—you see the ads in girlie magazines. But there's no way you're going to sit inside four walls with a pencil and paper and figure out how you're going to do something like get a statement from a transvestite on a murder case. You've got to react to the situation. No book is going to give you the self-discipline to hear some nut drone on for two hours as you wait for the right piece of information, or the patience to sit in a car all night when it's ten below."

Lewis got into the business in his twenties after a short stint as an insurance adjustor and received the experience needed for a license by doing investigations for a local attorney named Frank Bellotti who subsequently became the state attorney general. Typically, Lewis refused to join Bellotti's staff for fear it would compromise his independence. Instead he rented his own office one flight up, a dreary little place with green walls that was barely big enough for his desk, two folding chairs, and a filing cabinet.

Lewis now works out of his brown, shingled house in the Boston suburb of Wollaston. There's a view of the city off the deck out back and a spacious, but little-used yard. Inside, a rust-colored shag carpet covers the floor, and Lewis has an assortment of well-stuffed furniture. Divorced after a long, unsatisfying marriage, and out of touch with his three grown children, he lives here alone. A fluffy Pekingese named Mr. Moto—after the fictional Oriental detective—and dubbed Magoo used to keep him company, scampering about underfoot. But Lewis gave Magoo away because he felt he couldn't give the dog enough attention. A white cat named Grandma lurks about somewhere, out of sight. Lewis believes white cats bring him luck.

Solitude has become a habit for him; that, in simple terms, is why his marriage failed. "We were never able to talk things out, Nancy and me," he said. "It's odd in a way, since I'm so good at talking to people I don't know—witnesses, clients—and getting them to open up to me. But I could never bring myself to sit down with Nancy and talk about our problems. I think it's all those years alone in the car that made me that way. I just got used to holding everything in.

"I suppose I communicate to the people I'm closest to through my actions, not with words—by doing things for them. With my family, I was the protector and the provider. That was the way I expressed my love. Nancy never told me that wasn't enough, so I never knew. Even when we decided to get divorced, we never discussed the reasons for the breakup; we just did it. The communication just was never there."

Even without Nancy and the kids, the Wollaston residence still looks more like home than office. The only hints that this is also the headquarters of the Lewis Detective Agency are the framed license on the living-room wall and the sign on the heavy walnut desk saying WE DO THE FUCKING JOB. Lewis keeps his secret files in a safe in the next room, next to his barbells, and he hides the bullets to his gun up in the attic. He has his mail held at the post office so no one will break in to rifle it here at home. As a concession to the death threats he has received, he keeps the draperies drawn on the street side and positions his favorite reading chair back from the window. "You better have eyes in the back of your head, Lewis," an unknown voice once told him, "or you'll never know what hit you."

Lewis has one part-time associate at the agency, Roger Grove. He smokes a deep-bowl pipe and with his thick mop of gray hair and fondness for tweed, looks like an English schoolteacher. Although they've worked together for over a decade, Lewis doesn't know too much about Grove's background, except that he grew up in Illinois and is married. Lewis believes Grove holds down another job somewhere in Boston, but he doesn't know for sure, and doesn't *want* to know, for fear it may somehow compromise Grove's detective work.

The two meet to discuss the day's plans every morning over breakfast at the Wollaston Mug 'n' Muffin, a pleasant, brightly lit place where Lewis meets many of his clients. For mysterious reasons, the two call each other "Dickie" and engage in constant banter filled with lighthearted insults. To the boss's amusement, Grove always makes Lewis pay the check.

When they have to meet elsewhere later in the day, the two always play the same game with each other. Whichever arrives first, usually Lewis, will stand and wait at the appointed spot, and the other one will try to sneak up on him. "Roger's better at it than me," says Lewis. "If I'm waiting in a lobby someplace, I'll be watching all the entrances like a bastard and then I'll feel this tap on my shoulder and it'll be Roger. He'll come up the service entrance or down the elevator, or out of a phone booth or up a manhole. I never know where he's coming from."

Lewis never planned on hiring an associate, but Grove pestered him so continually about a job that finally the detective relented. "Now," he says, "I can't afford *not* to have him." Grove is the only man Lewis knows who has anything close to his own tolerance for twelve-hour stakeouts. Even better, he's proved a genius for extracting information over the phone. "If somebody calls you up saying he's a four-star general, or he's the Governor's press secretary," says Lewis admiringly, "it's probably Roger."

———

If the job ever held much glamour for Lewis, it's worn off by now. Most nights you can find him right where he is now—buried in the shadows of his car, waiting. He's slid over to the passenger seat, to make it look as if he's just waiting for the driver, should anyone spot him. He has also taken the precaution of lining up the car so that a fence post comes between his face and the front door of that house three numbers down. That way, if his client's husband were suddenly to emerge and take the quick, nervous look around that Lewis has come to expect from the guilty, he won't spot the detective. To vary things a bit in the last hour, he's pulled out of his spot to slide by the house and park at the other end of the street and watch the window through the rearview mirror. Perhaps later he'll check out another angle he's discerned through the trees from a couple of streets over. Lewis is being a touch more careful tonight than usual, for his client told him this afternoon that her husband has started carrying a handgun.

Inside Lewis' car, the air is thick with cigar smoke. Lewis switched over from cigarettes a while back when he realized that cigars don't burn quite so brightly when inhaled, and they last longer. He prefers Coronellas because they're cheap. Lewis shifts in his seat a few times as he watches, and he clears his throat quietly, but the sounds and movements are soft and infrequent, like twitches in his sleep.

"I'm a camera," he says. "I just watch and record what I see. I try to be untouched by it, because I need to be objective. Only the facts are any use. Without them, it's a never-never land of guesses and generalizations. My job is to find out what the facts are, and I lock them away in my head like a series of snapshots, ready to call them up when necessary. The reports that I write aren't eloquent or flowery. They're just memory jogs to call the images back to my head. And in my reports I never get into a moral discussion, saying how awful it is that some guy's sleeping around. I just keep it simple."

Still, as Lewis drifts through the night, he has come upon more than a few things that must have made him wonder. Patrolling down a cul-de-sac one night on surveillance, he discovered a police cruiser pulled up by an open window with its lights off. Looking closer, Lewis could see that the cop inside was masturbating to the sounds of a couple making love. On another case he followed a parish priest to a motel. Through the open shade, Lewis watched the priest undress himself, then disrobe a small boy, and, as the detective recalls, "the two of them started hopping all around the room in the nude like a couple of rabbits."

Lewis just watches. "If I thought too much about what I see, I'd jump off the Prudential Tower," he says, delivering his standard line on the subject. But it's not always easy to be a dispassionate observer, and some situations inevitably draw him in—like a certain night in the graveyard.

It was a terrible, rainy night before Halloween, and Lewis was staking the cemetery out from the greenhouse. Some vandals had been sneaking onto the property late at night to destroy equipment in the toolshed, crack tombstones, and smash the greenhouse windows. The police had investigated, but they hadn't been able to produce any leads. The graveyard owners had tried a special security firm that used guard dogs to protect the property, but the firm had backed out after finding four of its Doberman pinschers dead one morning with broken necks.

The owners turned to Lewis. "I figured it was a challenge," he says.

Lewis stationed another detective, Art Ross, in the car at the parking lot with a walkie-talkie while he and photographer Duane Smith (who would get shots of the culprits) watched from the greenhouse. A Southerner with a bit of redneck still in him, Smith brought along a pistol to protect himself. Lewis left his own guns behind, but he did borrow a massive and battle-scarred German shepherd named Fang from a dog breeder who owed him a favor. Lewis and Fang had spent the afternoon together getting acquainted.

"It was a bad night for a stakeout," Lewis remembers. "The rain was really coming down, and the wind was howling. The green-house windows were all fogged up and it was really dark out, but you could see something when the lightning flashed. Finally, around eleven o'clock, Duane was looking out toward the river, down past the gravestones, when there was a flash and he turns to me really scared and says, 'What the fuck is *that*?' I look and there's another flash and suddenly I see this thing about eight feet tall and four feet wide coming up from the river.

"I get a hold of Fang and crouch down. It's this enormous guy in a poncho and he's heading up for the toolshed. I'd had the owners put this big heavy iron gate over the door to secure it, but the guy just rips it off with his bare hands like a piece of cheese and charges in. Then there's this incredible noise inside. Blam! Smash! Pow! I see rakes and lawnmowers coming out the window. He must be tearing the place apart! Then he comes out again, and this time he comes straight for us.

"Now Duane's telling me, 'Did you hear that? Did you hear that?' but I'm trying to get Art on the walkie-talkie. 'Art,' I say; 'come in, Art!' but he doesn't answer. So I try to lift Fang up to the window so he can see the guy out there and attack him. I whisper, 'Ready!' in his ear like the trainer told me to, to get his attention, but all the dog does is squirm.

"The guy comes up closer and closer, and Duane's so terrified he just drops down on his hands and knees and backs away to the far end of the greenhouse like a crab. And Fang's shitless too. He starts whimpering and goes to hide under a table. This guy is huge! And he comes right up to the greenhouse door and picks up one of the tombstones stacked outside. He lifts it up over his head, really menacing, and I'm sure he's going to smash the place to bits, but I just brace myself and watch. And then—it's incredible, and I still don't know why he did it—he just crashes the tombstone down on the rest of the pile, blasting the whole slew of them to bits. Then he stalks off. I try to send Fang out to sniff around, but he won't budge, so I go out a few minutes later and check around, and the guy's gone. But I got a good description. I asked around later and found out he'd come up from a skiff on the river. The police found the guy. He had a history of mental illness, and his brother had just been fired as the graveyard's caretaker. I guess he wanted revenge."

———

It's typical that Lewis should have stayed hidden inside the whole time to see without being seen. "Distance," he says, "is always the answer." That's why, now, he stays a good distance down the street from the house he's watching, never out front. Tailing someone on the highway, he always hangs several cars back. He once staked out a lakeside apartment building by watching through a telescope a half-mile away across the water. To watch a beachfront estate, he anchored a fishing boat in the ocean, hung a fishing rod over the side, and peered at the house through a telescope hidden under a blanket. And to follow one roving husband on narrow, twisting country roads where Lewis knew he wouldn't be able to stay as far back as he needed to, the detective had the wife paint a white circle on the roof of the man's car and then went up in a hired plane to follow him from the sky.

But such extreme measures aren't always necessary and Lewis can do just fine by hovering in the middle distance, in the watery blur of people and things that fringes almost everyone's perceptions. "People look," he says, "but they don't see." They don't know what to look *for*. A key element in Lewis' favor is that however many private eyes a subject might have seen on television, no one ever believes *he* will be followed. "People are pretty trusting," he says. "Cops are tough to follow sometimes, because they're trained to be suspicious, and they can arrest you on the spot. And women sometimes cause problems. Not the beautiful ones, but the primpers, the ones who are always checking around to see who's interested. But mostly, people don't pay any attention to who's behind them."

As a result, Lewis can routinely pull off moves that would otherwise seem audacious. For instance, he finds he can walk into most people's living rooms just by knocking on the door with a clipboard in his hand and saying he's from the census. Or, to obtain an unlisted phone number for a client, he just parks his car in front of the house, throws his hood up and comes to the door wiping the grease from his hands. Then he explains that his car's broken down and asks if anyone would mind if he used the phone. The private number is printed right on it.

Roger Grove is more daring. Once, on an adultery case by a lake in the mountains, Grove walked right up to a couple he'd been following and handed them his camera.

"Would you be nice enough to take a picture of me by the lake?" he asked. "It's for my kids."

"Not at all," replied the man.

"Say," Grove went on after the shot, "how about if I took your picture too, as a memento?"

They didn't mind then, but they certainly had regrets later when the shot of the two of them, arms around each other's waists, faces beaming at the camera, was introduced as evidence at the divorce proceedings brought by the man's wife back home.

"Everybody has their own idea about what a private investigator looks like," Lewis declares, "and I don't fit the mold. Besides, the only thing people ever remember about a stranger is his hair and eyes." So his only disguise is the BMW baseball cap he's wearing now. By adjusting the plastic strap in the back, he can wear the cap a little higher on his head and become someone else. Sometimes, though, he'll affect a limp when following a subject into a restaurant. "People generally try not to stare at a cripple," he says, "and waiters give me prompt service. But you never want to stick out," he adds. "In this business it comes in pretty handy to have average looks and ordinary clothes."

Lewis has developed all kinds of talents to aid him in surveillance: he once took twelve lessons in ballroom dancing so he could follow his subject onto the dance floor without looking too conspicuous, and he's thinking of learning to ski for the same reason. He has also developed his peripheral vision so that he never has to watch his subject straight on in close quarters. "Direct is dangerous," he says. "Staring makes everybody uncomfortable, so I watch them out of the side of my eye. Or in a restaurant, where there are usually lots of mirrors, I'll use them. Out on the street, I use the plate-glass windows of banks and grocery stores, or the shiny sides of parked cars."

When Lewis does have to move in close to get a look at a man's face for verification, the detective always waits until the subject is

thoroughly distracted first. At a restaurant, for instance, his man will be busy going through his wallet to pay his bill when Lewis comes up to him to hand him a quarter and say, "I think you dropped this." Only when the man's eyes are on the coin will Lewis steal a look at his face. Then he'll quietly slip away.

If Lewis ever senses his subject's suspicions are aroused, he withdraws, but he always counts to ten before making any move. And he won't take up the chase again until he's "tested the waters" by drifting into the man's line of sight from at least fifty feet away. He watches in his peripheral vision for any reaction. Up close, though, if his man should ever stare at him as though trying to remember where he's seen Gil before, Lewis stares right back. "You can't let them back you down," he says, "or you look guilty."

With such techniques, Lewis has followed people for an entire year without their knowledge, and the realization hits them only when the case comes to trial. One woman fainted on the witness stand when Lewis gave her the word. "You couldn't imagine the look on her face," he says.

And now, finally, at a few minutes past three, the light in the bedroom window has finally blinked out. Lewis makes a note of the time on his legal pad and waits a few more minutes to make sure no one leaves the house. Then he crushes out his Coronella, cranks up the car one more time, and heads for home.

Despite the attempts to keep his distance on the case, though, Lewis has still become involved and he's still thinking about it when he arrives home, puts out some food for the cat, and undresses for bed. He's tallying the evidence, wondering where to position his car next time, reconsidering sight lines. He puts on the TV to distract himself and reaches for the remote-control button as he climbs into his double bed. With the remote control, he can turn the set off easily when, in an hour or so, he's finally nodding off. But even sleep brings no relief, for in his dreams he's back in his car again, gazing up at lighted windows along dark, silent streets.

"My clients are trying to climb out, but all the rungs are miss-
ing from the ladder. It's my job to put the rungs back. And to
do that I have to climb down with them into the pit."

TWO

Shots in the Dark

"I have to treat most of my clients like children," says Lewis
over his usual fried eggs at the Wollaston Mug 'n' Muffin. "Mine's
a hand-holding operation. When clients come to me, they're
frightened and confused because they've been lied to for so long
about what's really going on—by their husbands if it's a domestic
case, or maybe by the police. They're so mixed up I have to throw
out ninety percent of what they tell me. I've seen this time after
time. Galloping paranoia sets in and they start to suspect anybody
and everybody except, usually, the person who's actually responsible. There's no escape. They're trying to climb out, but all the
rungs are missing from the ladder. It's my job to put the rungs
back. And to do that I have to climb down with them into the pit."

Lewis pauses a moment to finish off his eggs, the only meal he'll
have today—he'll rely on coffee, vitamin pills, Stresstabs, and
quick-energy Go Ahead bars to get him the rest of the way. Then
he dabs at the corner of his mouth with his napkin, leans forward,
and modulates into the quieter, softer key he reserves for personal
confidences.

He wants to talk about Elaine Noble. A state representative
from Boston, she displayed many of the classic symptoms of the

helpless client when she turned to Gil Lewis in February of 1976. By coincidence, Lewis had seen her a few nights before on Tom Snyder's *Tomorrow* show. He'd been impressed with how calm and controlled she seemed. But when she called him up, she sounded almost hysterical as she recounted wild stories about a gang of terrorists who were bombing her car, blowing out her apartment windows, and ringing her phone off the hook with threatening calls.

Lewis arranged to meet her at nine sharp the next morning.

Always punctual, the detective buzzed at Noble's door a little ahead of time, just to be on the safe side. The place was a shabby brownstone in a part of the Back Bay that's populated mostly by college students. Lewis couldn't help noticing that Noble's downstairs bay windows had been broken and were covered with cardboard.

Noble looked relieved to see the detective, dressed in his usual blue jeans and leather jacket and working a Coronella between his teeth. An attractive woman with black hair and satin skin, she ushered Lewis into her living room, which, going by the Oriental rugs and porcelain vases, the detective sized up as "old money." Seated pensively on the couch was a woman who could have been Noble's twin. It was her roommate and lover, Rita Mae Brown, the author, Lewis happened to know, of the best-selling *Rubyfruit Jungle* and other books about lesbianism. There were also a gaunt, fluttery woman named Meg Sinclair, and two others. All of them, it seemed, had been caught up in the violence that was aimed at Noble.

"Like I say," Lewis repeats, "they all seemed just like frightened kids. That surprised me, because these were people of power. But they were all staring at me wide-eyed and sitting on the edge of their chairs." To loosen them up, Lewis took off his leather jacket and very deliberately laid it over the back of his chair, then sat back down, stretching his legs out in front of him. "I try to come across as super-relaxed—that can be just as contagious as paranoia," he observes. But when they finally started in, all five of the women got talking at once.

Normally Lewis takes no notes during an interview for fear it will distract his clients, but this time he had to reach quickly for his legal pad. To begin with, there were threatening phone calls—thousands of them. Rita Mae Brown got most, since she was home writing—or trying to—most of the day while Noble was at the State House. They came at all hours—sometimes, incredibly, as often as forty times a day. The callers had a variety of voices, both male and female, and identified themselves with more than a dozen different names. The threats were vicious and bizarre. Sometimes simply "We're gonna get you." Click. Other times the callers would tell Rita what she was wearing: "Nice red blouse you have on, Rita," they'd say, as if they were watching her at that very moment. Terrified, Brown would run to the windows, but she could never spot anybody looking in.

And then the threats became reality. Somebody shot Rita's beautiful Audi full of bullets and, not long after, blew out the windows in Elaine's Chevy Vega. The two had their cars repaired only to find their gas tanks filled with sugar. Once Noble discovered while driving that the lug bolts had been loosened in one front wheel, almost causing her to swerve off the road. At home, the terrorists were blowing out the apartment windows with alarming

regularity. One morning, while Brown was there alone, they blew holes through both the front and back windows of the apartment with a pellet gun, scattering glass everywhere and scaring Brown out of her wits. The callers were always quick to claim responsibility. "Too bad about your car, Rita," they'd snicker, or "Sorry about the windows."

Meg Sinclair added that she too had gotten a number of crank calls; other friends of Elaine's had found their cars shot up or spray-painted; and still others received threats that their children would be kidnapped or their dogs shot. One had even awakened to the sounds of firemen breaking into her house. They said they'd received a call that the building was on fire.

"It's as if anyone who gets close to me gets *zinged*," Noble said. It had gotten to the point where she suspected everyone. She joked, nervously, that she hardly knew whether she could trust everybody right here in this room. The police had been so unhelpful, she'd come to think that maybe they were behind the campaign against her. From the very start Noble had reported every incident, but the police merely recorded each one as it occurred, denying any connection between them. Once some of the cops came by after a shooting episode at the apartment and collected a few pellets from the living-room floor. They left telling the two "not to worry" and that was all. Noble knew that her lawyer, Nancy Gertner, also represented the radical bank robbers Susan Saxe and Kathy Power. Saxe had turned herself in the summer before, but Power was still high on the FBI's most-wanted list. Could the police be hoping to scare the women into revealing Power's hideout?

Lewis made notes for three hours in his loopy, backward-slanting script. When the five women finally ran out of horrors, they shifted their eyes to the detective with the look of expectation he sees in every client the first time. The look says: Well, there you have it. Now it's your problem—what are you doing to do?

"I knew there would be no fast answers," says the detective. "It was all so wild! But I was sure that with so many incidents, some incriminating evidence would emerge. I told the women what to do. From now on, when these calls come in, I told them to try to keep the callers on the line to get as many personal details out of them as possible. I also told them to pull the shades on all their windows. And to get a clear story out of this welter, I told them to put together a list of everything that had happened to them in chronological order. Meanwhile, I'd go down to the phone company to get a trace put on Noble's line to find out where the calls were coming from. Frankly, I was surprised the police hadn't done that already."

The five thanked Lewis profusely as he left. And for the first time in a while, they all slept peacefully that night. Back in Wollaston, however, Lewis was awakened at two in the morning by a call on his unlisted line. "We saw you at Elaine's today," said a high-pitched male voice. "Don't be stupid. Stay out of this or we'll take care of you."

Caught out for the moment, Lewis simply hung up. He has gotten his share of threatening calls. "Most of them," he says, "telling me they're going to blow my head off. I don't pay much attention. Killers strike out on impulse, they don't call beforehand." But now he lay awake for a while, wondering what he'd gotten himself into this time.

———

After a week of private interviews with Noble and her friends, Lewis began to get a sense of the pattern of violence and even discerned a couple of leads. The only name that the callers used with any regularity was Al Armbrister. Lewis decided to run it by his friends at the Registry of Motor Vehicles—contacts established through favors early in Lewis' career and kept in good working order with generous Christmas presents ever since. And he put his associate Roger Grove on it.

The other lead was more complicated, but seemed more promising. Just after Brown's Audi was shot up, a message had come in on Noble's answering machine from a Dr. Janet Williams asking Rita to call her back on extension 203 at the Massachusetts General Hospital in downtown Boston. When Brown returned the call, a kind-sounding woman answered and told Brown she had been in a coin laundry off Marlborough when she saw someone shooting at the Audi from a passing car. Dr. Williams said she couldn't see who it was, but had written down the vandal's license-plate number, which she now read off to Brown. The two chatted on for a while about Brown's books, which Williams said she just *loved,* and

33

then hung up. Brown passed the information on to the police, but after checking with the registry, the cops reported back that there was no such plate number in circulation.

It was only then that Brown realized that this Dr. Williams hadn't explained how she had known to reach her at Elaine's— hardly anybody knew Rita was living there. For that matter, Williams hadn't said how she knew the Audi was Brown's. Frantic, Rita tried to call the doctor back. This time, at extension 203, no one had ever heard of Dr. Janet Williams. And later, Brown thought she recognized Dr. Williams' voice as that of one of the crank callers. She was more scared than ever.

To Lewis, though, this was the case's biggest break. It meant somebody at the MGH *had* to be involved.

The next morning Lewis drove out to the MGH, a massive collection of stubby, 1950s-drab buildings all clustered haphazardly around a single tower. After parking in the garage, Lewis sidestepped the knots of anxious visitors in the waiting room and found the door listing SENIOR ADMINISTRATOR HARVEY FIELD, M.D.

Field's office was spacious and decorated with flowers and an expensive-looking oil painting. Lewis sensed he was in for trouble, and sure enough, Field treated the detective as though he had a communicable disease. "Field was a real song-and-dance man," says Lewis. "But I'm used to dealing with tap dancers and I can handle their patter. I knew just how to handle Field."

When Field tried to evade the detective's questions by saying that at least twenty people must have access to extension 203 and that Mr. Lewis couldn't possibly want to investigate them all . . . Lewis cut him off short. "Why don't you let me handle that?" he snapped. "Just give me the names."

A half-hour later Lewis had the list, and there were precisely two people on it: Henry LeBeau and Irving Drinker. Apparently, extension 203 rang in a spare technicians' office in the Urology Department; the room was usually locked and only those two had keys. Asked about them, Field said only that LeBeau lived "somewhere in the suburbs" and Drinker had recently moved to the Back Bay. The Back Bay connection caught the detective's attention, but he didn't let on. He just thanked Field gruffly and left.

That night Lewis took Elaine Noble for a drive out to the end of

Newbury Street, where the Chinese laundries take over from the chichi boutiques and galleries, to pay an unexpected call on Irving Drinker. He thought Noble might recognize him, and he told her to give a signal by rubbing her eye if she did. When no one answered their buzz, Lewis and Noble returned to his car to wait.

Even though Lewis thinks of himself as a loner, he does like company from time to time. Since romantic entanglements with clients are nothing but trouble in his business, Lewis had no designs on Elaine Noble, and felt reassured that, as a lesbian, she would have none on him in return. Nevertheless, as he does with all women, he called her "dear" and, between puffs on his Coronella, met her brown eyes with his. Noble was touched by his old-fashioned gallantry, and as the two waited together in the front seat of his Buick, she gradually opened up to him.

She was really afraid she was losing her mind, she said. As an active liberal and openly gay politician, she'd faced some scary situations before. At an antibusing rally one time, a teen-ager had pointed a loaded shotgun at her head. But this was different. This had gone on for two whole years, and no one understood what she was going through. When she told her State House colleagues about her troubles, they just passed it off as the usual razzing all politicians have to put up with. Her nonpolitical friends were even less supportive, claiming that, with her connections as a pol, she could stop the violence if she really wanted to. But she didn't dare tell many people, for fear the newspapers would get wind of the story and bring the craziness down on her all the harder.

Scared as she was for herself, she was even more afraid of what was happening to Rita. Elaine had taken to concealing some of the damage, getting car windows replaced without her lover's knowing. But even so, Rita was turning against her, threatening to follow the advice of friends and move out.

Were people objecting to her gayness? Her politics? Were the police behind the terrorism because of that Saxe and Power thing? Could it be a political opponent? Or just some weirdos? Whoever it was, Noble wished they would just stop.

Gil reassured her that he was making progress, but in the light of an oncoming car, he could see that her eyes were glistening with tears.

Finally, a young man in a lumber jacket came up the sidewalk

35

and let himself into the apartment building. It was Drinker. Lewis and Noble followed. Drinker, in his early twenties, had a beard, thinning hair, and a distracted, edgy manner, and he did not seem happy to receive these two unexpected visitors, although he let them in. Art prints were taped to the peeling walls of his apartment and a large stack of medical journals were piled in one corner. Drinker's calico cat jumped into Noble's lap as she and Lewis sat down on the sagging couch.

Lewis explained about the harassment calls to Noble's apartment from extension 203. Drinker eyed the state rep. suspiciously. "I've been wanting to meet you," he said. Lewis had told Noble to give a signal by rubbing her eye if she recognized Drinker's voice, but she kept her hands by her side. She stroked the cat, and spoke only to inform Drinker that his pet had ear mites, and that he should daub its ears with olive oil.

Lewis cleared his throat and reached for a Coronella in his breast pocket. "We're talking to everybody who had access to that phone," he said. "Routine questions—just like the police asked."

"The cops haven't talked to me," Drinker replied.

Lewis would have to verify that one, but it made him think that Noble might be right—the police didn't want to solve the case. "The Drinker lead was so basic," he says.

Although Drinker claimed to have lived on Newbury Street for over a year, he could provide only one name as a neighborhood reference—Irene Powell. "She's a lawyer for the Ford Foundation," he added proudly. Then he turned to Noble. "She's never approved of you, y'know."

Lewis let that one pass also, preferring to keep the conversation rolling. "You find out more if you just let them ramble," he says. "They hang themselves if you give them enough rope." And sure enough, Drinker talked on and on, at last boasting about how much overtime he worked in the urology lab, and yes, he could have been there on the Saturday this Dr. Williams called. But, suddenly defensive, Drinker insisted he didn't know anything about that. "I bet Maria Valdez is your girl," he said. "That sounds like something she'd do. She's a Jesus freak—you know, really wild."

Far from shifting Lewis' attention, the remark just made Lewis all the more suspicious of the young man before him. "That's a dead giveaway," he explains. "People who have something to hide always try to push me off onto somebody else."

As Lewis got up to leave, he asked Drinker if he could use the phone.

"Don't have one," Drinker answered.

Lewis figured that extension 203 was getting a lot of use.

Outside, Noble couldn't wait to tell him what she knew about Irene Powell. She was a woman who'd weaseled her way into Noble's '74 campaign claiming, falsely, to be a Washington attorney. Noble had had her checked out after Powell suggested spray-painting VOTE NOBLE all over her opponent's headquarters windows.

———

Lewis found Drinker's colleague Harry LeBeau examining urine samples in the lab a few days later. LeBeau was chubby and wore very thick glasses. "There must be a dozen people who have keys to that room," he replied irritably to Lewis' first question.

"Who uses it the most?"

"That would probably be Irving."

"Irving Drinker?"

"That's right. Don't worry about him, though; he's harmless."

To get a better sense of LeBeau, Lewis drove out to look over his house. It was a ranch-style suburban with a station wagon in the driveway and a rectangular swimming pool out back. "I could see I was dealing with a typical suburban mentality," says Lewis. "This was a guy who didn't want to rock any boat." So much for LeBeau.

Lewis also investigated Maria Valdez, the woman Drinker had fingered, but when Lewis called her supervisors at the MGH they spoke too highly of her to allow much room for suspicion. He interviewed her anyway, but could see that even the Jesus-freak description was in her favor. She was just "too anemic."

By now, Roger Grove had turned up two Al Armbristers through the registry. The first was a black short-order cook living in Mattapan. After following the man for a couple of days and asking a few discreet questions, Grove concluded the genial burger chef wasn't the threatening type.

Al Armbrister number two lived in Milton and turned out to be a retired Back Bay building superintendent. He'd never heard of Drinker, but when Grove mentioned Irene Powell, Armbrister said he could remember her distinctly: a short, blubbery woman who'd been a tenant in his building several years back. Grove could see that Armbrister was too old for phone pranks, but Powell could easily have borrowed her old super's name as an alias for Drinker.

Lewis decided it was time to check further into the Drinker–Powell connection. Interviewing more of Drinker's co-workers, Lewis found that the lab technician had received a job offer from the Ford Foundation. Another said she'd seen Drinker leave the lab a few times arm in arm with a couple of thirtyish women. And an old roommate, whom Lewis tracked down through Drinker's Newbury Street superintendent, told the investigator that Drinker was "gun-happy" and that in his modest collection he had a pellet gun. The case was beginning to fall into place.

The hang-up calls to Noble and her friends were now jangling the wires around the clock. The callers seemed to be getting riled up. Worse, Lewis discovered from the phone log the women had compiled for him that an increase in phone calls had always led to an outbreak of vandalism. Despite Lewis' efforts, the phone company had yet to put on a trace, so he was still far from proving that those "zingers," as Noble called them, were coming from extension 203—or anywhere else. The five did their best to draw the callers out, as Lewis had instructed, but the pranksters never let anything slip.

Determined to get something conclusive on Drinker before any worse damage was done, Lewis had Noble call the technician at the MGH while Rita Mae Brown and Meg Sinclair listened on extension phones. At Lewis' suggestion, Noble told Drinker that she was just calling to make sure his cat was all right. Drinker seemed surprised and a little touched by her interest. "Oh, she's fine," he replied They went on about cats awhile more, then hung up.

Afterward, Brown spoke for everyone: "That's Armbrister."

Sitting on the living-room couch with the three women gathered around him, Lewis took a deep, satisfied drag on his Coronella and pondered the situation. What could the lab technician have against Elaine Noble? He seemed strange, all right, but not *nasty*. His friend Irene Powell, however, from the little Lewis had heard about her, seemed a good deal of both. On a hunch, Lewis asked Noble to dial the number Drinker had given them for Powell while Sinclair and Brown went back to the upstairs phones.

Powell answered on the third ring. Noble was direct with her, explaining about the prank calls and asking if she knew Irving Drinker. "Vaguely," replied the woman. She didn't elaborate, on that or any other subject. Still, her few words were enough to convince Brown that she had heard, once again, the voice of Dr. Janet Williams.

Lewis had been on the case exactly ten days. And now he was ready to move into the phase of the investigation that he could do best. It might take another few weeks—the long process of gathering evidence; tracking the suspects until he could catch them in the act of making a call, shooting up an apartment, blasting a car. It was just a matter of time.

Now that he had Powell's phone number, Lewis wouldn't even have to wait for that trace. He gave the number to his contacts in the billing department at the phone company and found it belonged not to Irene Powell, but to another woman, Christine Stakowski, in the Fenway. He staked out her place that night.

Lewis asked Noble along for the ride, hoping she'd be able to pick out Powell. Duane Smith, the photographer he uses for shots he doesn't trust to his Instamatic, came too. Smith goes all out for Lewis' cases, packing special lenses and infrared film to photograph illicit lovers by starlight. Tonight, though, Lewis told him to stick to regular black-and-white film and a zoom lens.

Stakowski's was a big brick apartment building, with tiers of bay windows across the front. Lewis had sneaked into the building earlier that afternoon—by carrying a bag of groceries up to the front door and waving his keys just as an elderly man was letting himself in—and found Stakowski's apartment, number eight, on the third floor, street side. The light was on now, as the three watched from Lewis' car, but the shades were drawn. Noble was pleased to have turned the tables on her tormentors. Now she was spying on *them*.

Finally, around ten, the apartment lights snapped off and, moments later, two heavyset women emerged. They both wore parkas, which made them look even heavier. Watching them, Noble started to squirm. "That's them! That's them!" she yelled.

Lewis hushed her and waited till the pair turned the corner before starting the car to follow them. By the time he'd caught up, the couple had stepped into a pizza joint. Lewis pulled up out front for the photographs, but Smith claimed it was an impossible shot—through all that glass, and there wasn't enough light. But Noble grabbed the camera. "I'll operate this sucker," she said, and got six shots before Lewis had to drive off.

———

Was Lewis excited to see the people he'd thought about practically around the clock for nearly two weeks? "I was *interested* in seeing them, sure," he says, "but only because I knew I was going to have to place them under surveillance for a long period of time. I wanted to see what they looked like, how they moved, what places they frequented. I always want to put a face on the name. But excitement, that's anathema to me."

Lewis was even more interested when Elaine's pictures were developed—and one showed in the enlargement something no one had noticed: the two women were holding hands under the table. They were gay!

When Noble saw the pictures, she felt faint. What could these two women, who *should* have been on her side, have against her?

She'd never seen them before in her life, but still they'd followed her every move, tormenting her in every possible way, for two whole years. Why?

Desperate for answers, she and her friend Meg Sinclair decided to do some surveillance of their own. Without telling Gil, Noble and Sinclair waited outside Powell's apartment in Sinclair's VW microbus one evening until Powell and Stakowski drove off in a battered gray Toyota. They followed for miles as the Toyota wound all around the city, dipping into side streets only to head off down the wide avenues, and finally pulling into a dark alley in the South end. Noble nosed the VW in after them. Suddenly Powell jumped out from the darkness and charged at them. "What the fuck are you following us for?" she screamed. "Get out of here!" Noble shoved the VW into reverse, but Sinclair jumped out at the hefty Powell and started grappling with her. Both women were screaming, and before long the police appeared to pull the two women apart and tell everybody to go on home.

When Lewis heard about this, he could see why Noble and Sinclair had wanted to take matters into their own hands, but he was still upset. He felt they'd really screwed things up, just when the case was turning his way. Now he'd have to lie back for a while, waiting for things to cool down. Powell and Stakowski knew they were being followed, and they'd do anything to avoid getting caught.

Shortly after the ruckus, the telephone company had finally put a tracer on Noble's line. It was spitting out a stack of computer cards for all the crank calls, showing numbers of pay phones all around the city, and although Lewis wouldn't normally have had any trouble shadowing the pair, waiting for that one false move, in the following weeks he had no luck. He stayed right on them, but he never saw any action. "They must have waited till there were no cars in sight before making the calls," he says. "They weren't trusting *anyone*." Noble reported that no calls came in while Lewis was on surveillance. But the phone kept ringing at other times. The detective received one call himself. "Relax, Lewis," said a voice, "we were only kidding about Noble. Lay off—this is just a prank."

Lewis didn't want to lay off before getting the photos he'd need to finalize Noble's case against the Powell threesome. But the three

41

had acted so skittish since the brawl in the South End that Lewis felt, for everybody's sake, he'd better go ahead with what he had.

He wrote a detailed fifteen-page report to the Major Violators division of the D.A.'s Office, a department recently established to speed up the prosecution of murderers, rapists, and other major felons. Impressed by the severity of the threats and the violence committed against Noble and her friends, Assistant D.A. Peter McCray summoned Drinker, Powell, and Stakowski before Judge Abrams at the Pemberton Square Courthouse three weeks later. Abrams seemed to listen intently to McCray's presentation of the case against the trio, but in the end he gave them a sentence that seemed to Lewis like "something out of the Wild West." Abrams ordered Drinker to pack up and get out of town. Case closed.

Noble was stuck in a session at the State House during the hearing. But that afternoon she got a call from a hysterical Rita Mae Brown who shouted that while she was working upstairs, someone had broken into the Marlborough Street apartment. She came down to find the glass on the front door broken, a potted plant smashed, and the door to Elaine's study wide open. Inside, nothing had been touched except one of the filing cabinets: a drawer was pulled out and the folder containing Noble's records on the case was gone. It had happened while Drinker, Stakowski, and Powell were in court.

When Noble got home, she found a moving van in front of the house. "I'm out of here, Elaine," Rita Mae told her. "It's all over."

———

Whether it was Brown's departure or Drinker's—Elaine would never know—the calls stopped as mysteriously as they had begun.

Lewis dropped his investigation and Noble carried on in the Marlborough Street apartment alone, and felt no danger.

Six months later, as Noble was gearing up for what she knew would be her last state-rep. campaign, a short, hefty woman approached her at the South End Community Center headquarters. "I'm Irene Powell," announced the woman. "I just wanted to apologize for everything we put you through."

At first Noble just stared. Then she replied, her voice trembling, "If you wanted to destroy everything that had any meaning for me, you accomplished a lot. This is my last state-rep. campaign. I'll probably never get in front of anything again. My friends all hate me. Rita's moved out. I may lose all my property. And you say you're sorry. Tell me—why the hell did you do it?"

"It just looked like you had everything going for you," Powell answered, her jealousy still strong. "You were gay, but you were really making it. It just didn't seem right."

Elaine called Lewis with the story, but by that time the detective was puzzling the morality of the case from a different angle. He'd submitted his bill for the case: $430, covering the time Grove had spent tracking the two Armbristers. Beneath an itemization of Grove's fee, the detective put: "Gil Lewis—57 hours at $25.00 per hour—no charge." In the course of the investigation, he explains, he'd found out that Noble, like most politicians, was severely strapped for cash, and he decided, as he often does, to do the work for no charge. His lucrative domestic cases would make up for it. And to keep from embarrassing Noble, he'd listed only half his hours. Even so, he never did get full payment for Roger. He had to make up the difference himself.

But Lewis shrugs this off. "Every case where you don't take a sizable retainer you take that chance," he says. "I'm a big boy. If I worried about the money, I'd be running a variety store." Others might express regret about doing so much work for so little pay— not Lewis. "I never expect to make money on a pol," he says. And he never sent her a second bill. Still, he was distressed by the police department's lack of interest in the whole affair. No doubt the cops had strung Noble out to get at the radicals Saxe and Power. But, Lewis had to ask himself, what was *he* getting out of all this? He wondered about that one a long time.

"I just assumed that if I could keep awake I could do any-thing."

THREE

This Way Out

When Gil Lewis was two years old, he came down with a case of pneumonia that so weakened the muscles behind his right eye that the pupil rolled in toward his nose and practically disappeared. It took years of special eye exercises with the ophthalmologist to correct the condition. It's still not quite perfect. Sitting across from you, he can look into your left eye with his right and into your right with his left at the same time.

Lewis believes that all the time spent trying to blend the two colored bars together in the viewer as a child helped develop his concentration. His eye trouble also earned him a reputation as a "brain," since he had to read a lot to strengthen his eye muscles. At eight, impatient with all the words he didn't know, he claims he read the entire dictionary. When he grew older, the flashy vocabulary began to work against him, and it was largely to defend himself from the bullying he received as a cross-eyed child with bookish tastes that he started boxing and lifting weights.

Lewis was not particularly happy at home. He grew up in Wollaston, just a few blocks from the house where he would ultimately raise his own family, and always felt squeezed as the fourth of seven children. To get away, Gil moved his bed up to the attic, although the heat up there was so bad in the summers that he sometimes had to sleep with his head on the windowsill. He remembers he spent most of his spare time alone looking for driftwood on Wollaston Beach.

Eager to escape, Lewis enlisted in the Air Force on the morning of his eighteenth birthday. He hoped to fly away from his troubles as the pilot of a thundering F-86, but that possibility evaporated as soon as Airman Lewis' commanding officers got the results of his eye test. They wouldn't even let him crew. Impressed by the scores on his IQ test, however, they packed him off to a cartography school where he pasted together maps based on aerial photographs taken by pilots, an irony the earthbound Lewis found maddening. An inept cartographer—he might have been wearing boxing gloves, he had so little grace in drawing those sinuous lines—he was finally put to work hand-lettering signs like KEEP OFF THE GRASS, OFFICERS ONLY, and THIS WAY OUT.

Securing a transfer to a communications center on the eastern tip of Long Island, Lewis volunteered to shimmy up 110-foot, rickety wooden poles to repair the radar equipment on top. It meant teetering in the wind for hours at a time, secured only by long spikes on his shoes and a leather belt around his waist. "But up there," he says, "no one could give me orders." He spent two years at it. Once, when his boot spike hit a patch of dry rot, he slid twenty-five feet, catching a splinter that went right through his hand. He was discharged after four years.

——

One of the first things Lewis did when he returned to Wollaston was get engaged to golden-haired Nancy Ward, who, everyone said, looked just like Gil's mother. Gil himself didn't see the resemblance, although he had noticed that his mother warmed to Nancy right away. He felt he'd finally found a woman who appreciated him. On Halloween, 1956, the couple were married in a small ceremony in St. Peter's chapel in Dorchester.

While Nancy was cheerful and kind and much softer than the women he'd dated in the Air Force, it quickly became clear that Lewis wasn't ready for a wife. For one thing, although Lewis had hoped his years in the service would improve his employment prospects, he ended up with his old job stuffing bags into Greyhound buses. Because of his meager income, the newlyweds were forced to move in with Nancy's mother. Lewis started moonlighting driving delivery trucks—partly, he now thinks, just to stay out of the house. And, accustomed to working long hours, he found it easy to include classes at Suffolk University, all paid for by the GI Bill. He dreamed of someday becoming an attorney. In school, Lewis did well in English and his prelaw courses—but one night another talent emerged.

On weekends after dinner he used to study the statute books by himself in the law library at the Quincy Courthouse, a wonderfully quiet place with mahogany paneling and high ceilings. Most nights, Lewis was the only one in the whole building except the janitor, a likable guy he knew only as Joe.

Lewis had an Indian's awareness of his surroundings even then, and on this winter night as he labored over his books, he realized that although he'd heard Joe go shuffling down the hall promptly at ten for his evening rounds, there had been no sound of him since, and it was past eleven. Alarmed, Lewis went to the window and looked out. In the new-fallen snow, two fresh sets of footprints led around to a back window. That was odd, particularly since he remembered that the snow had been untouched when he came in at nine. Suspicious, he clicked off the lights and was about to go downstairs to investigate when he heard footsteps and low voices outside in the hall. He barely had time to hide behind the door before two men burst in. Lewis held his breath.

The intruders looked inside, saw that the lights were off, then went out again. "The guy must've gone," Lewis could hear one of them say as their footsteps died away down the hall. He waited a few moments, then crept out after them toward the stairs, his only way out. Gingerly he inched down the wooden stairs step by step and had almost reached the ground floor when, with a frightful clatter, two men in grotesque Halloween masks dashed up from the basement to confront him. One, in a gorilla face, pointed a shotgun at Lewis' head. The Frankenstein monster, right behind, carried an acetylene tank. Without stopping to think, Lewis went right into action. He yelled out, "Okay, Frank," to an imaginary person somewhere behind him, "you go around the front, Al, you take the back. Tell the others to close in."

The two masked men froze for a moment, then dashed off in separate directions while Lewis sprinted for the front door. He hadn't quite made it down the hall when he heard one of them yell, "Hey! That guy's full of shit! He's *alone!*" Racing back, the ape-man tried to level his shotgun at Lewis but slid on the linoleum and careened into a wall as Lewis burst through the front door.

Safely outside, Lewis hid in the bushes. When no one came after him, he ran to a bar down the street and called the police. They roared up minutes later, sirens blaring, in a half-dozen cruisers, surrounded the courthouse, and grabbed the two thugs.

When Lewis read about his heroism in the papers the next morning, he learned the intruders had been trying to blow up the safe in the basement to steal their arrest records. They'd tied Joe up and locked him in a basement cell and had been threatening to blow his brains out when they heard Lewis on the stairs. If they'd succeeded at the courthouse, they told reporters, they were plotting an assault on the police station. But the twenty-six-year-old law student had foiled their plans.

———

In the wake of his celebrity, Lewis signed on as a campaign aide with Wollaston attorney Frank Bellotti in his '59 campaign for D.A. And two years later, when Bellotti made his bid for Lieutenant governor, he hired Lewis to run his whole campaign up to the midsummer convention, when he knew the party would insist the pros take over. Lewis was still laboring over his books at Suffolk and his bags at Greyhound, but "I had to take that job," he recalls. "It was such a good opportunity. And I just assumed if I kept awake I could do anything."

By now, with three growing children to support, Lewis was very hard pressed financially. He learned of openings for liability adjustors in the insurance business, and as soon as the election was over and Bellotti was the Lieutenant Governor, Lewis rushed to apply for one of the jobs. The full-time insurance work meant abandoning Suffolk and his dream of becoming a lawyer; but the move also meant an end to his "heavy shoes and lunch pail" routine at Greyhound, and he felt, with his money worries, that he had little choice.

Best of all, he soon earned enough to make a $300 down payment on a tiny tract house in suburban Norwell, located, appropriately, on Nancy Lane. The place was practically all roof, and it looked like an overturned dinghy, but it was all his. To Lewis, the only problem was that although the ocean was just eight miles away, in a better section of town, the development was built on a sunken sand pit, so there was never any breeze.

When Lewis noticed that the neighbors all had dogs, he made an uncharacteristic stab at conformity by buying one too—a German shepherd named Bruno, who never came when he was called. After spending most of his work time trying to track down witnesses, Lewis would come home and have to spend hours more hunting for Bruno.

As an adjustor, Lewis investigated automobile smashups and other accident claims, to determine how much his company owed. Although his colleagues advised him to rely on the police accident reports, Lewis insisted on driving out to look over the area, examine the wreckage, locate witnesses, interview police officers, and generally figure out what had happened for himself. He saw some pretty gruesome sights—heads plucked off in truck collisions, chests pierced by steering columns, or throats sawed open on broken windshields—but for Lewis, dealing with the lawyers was the worst part, partly because he knew he would never be one of them. Once when he was waiting to settle a claim with an attorney, Lewis overheard the man tell someone on the phone that he knew how to handle adjustors: "Give them a bottle of booze and they're yours forever." Lewis spotted a new bottle of Canadian Club on the desk as he walked in, and didn't give the attorney a chance to speak. "You can stick that bottle right up your ass!" he yelled. "You can't buy me. I'm never coming here again." Then Lewis walked out. It took two years to settle that claim.

The insurance companies themselves, though, were little better. One adjustor got special praise for whittling down to $150 the claim of a destitute woman who'd been shot in the eye with a bow and arrow. So when Bellotti returned to private practice in 1964 and invited Lewis to do investigations for him in the criminal field, Gil was only too happy to oblige. It would be pretty much the same work he'd done with the insurance company—just establishing the facts by examining evidence and interviewing witnesses. The two agreed that Lewis would maintain his independence by working out of a separate office one flight up.

After three years of investigating nothing but car wrecks, Lewis found rape, embezzlement, robbery, and murder intriguing. He still had an academic reaction to things, and he spent long hours puzzling over these crimes, pondering motivations, relationships, methods. It started to bother Nancy, the way his mind was so wrapped up in his cases. He'd stay up late at night thinking about them.

He played his cases in his mind like solitaire, only it was more than a game. Lives now hung on Lewis' work: a satisfying development for a man whose own life had been toyed with so often by others—at home, in the military, and in the insurance business. Making phone calls, tracking down witnesses, interviewing, he sometimes imagined himself digging for buried treasure. For him, truth had that kind of inherent value. It made him feel rich.

Bellotti was the sort of person who never dished out compliments. If you were doing good work, he just gave you more of it. After three years, Lewis was up to his eyeballs in Bellotti cases. And the two genuinely liked each other. Lewis had sold Bellotti on his nutritional regimen. Bellotti had looked the other way when Lewis' temper occasionally flared up. As Bellotti advanced toward the state Attorney General's office, the two men stayed close, attending each other's private birthday parties, getting together for family outings, and fundamentally, each of them finding the other worthy of his trust—as rare in political circles as it is in detective work.

Nevertheless, Lewis was, after three years, getting a little tired of playing humble Paul Drake to Bellotti's shrewd Perry Mason, and wanted to strike out on his own. He knew his experience qualified him under Massachusetts statute for a private investigator's licence. When Lewis broached the subject, Bellotti was surprisingly obliging and just reached into his wallet for three $100 bills to pay Lewis' application fee. Three weeks later, the license arrived in the mail—an eight-by-ten document, badly reproduced and laden with signatures and blotchy seals. It looked a little like a certificate of membership in some teen idol's fan club. Lewis framed it proudly anyway and mounted it on his wall.

But he still had no clients. There was no way to leave the Bellotti roost just yet. First he needed to crack a headline case to establish his reputation. And that kind hadn't been coming Bellotti's way. His cases had been juicy, frightening, wild, but all small-town stuff, not the kind that wins an investigator any attention.

Then on July 9, 1967, a Weymouth policeman was arrested for manslaughter.

"The police department is a fraternal organization only in the best of times. When you fuck up, you fuck up on your own."

FOUR

On His Own

It was the late sixties, and every newspaper in the Northeast went wild over the story of twenty-five-year-old Wayne Nugent, killer cop. Frank Bellotti was to be the rookie patrolman's defense attorney. He put Lewis on the case as private investigator.

When Lewis met Nugent a few days later in his office, he was amazed at the similarity between the two of them. Like Lewis, Nugent was muscular, young, brown-eyed, and had tousled hair that came to a pronounced V on his forehead; he even lifted weights every morning—or at least, he *had* until his arrest. Now Nugent didn't feel he had the strength. His appetite was shot, and bags were starting to form under his hollow eyes—not surprising, considering the short life expectancy of a cop in jail. An idealist, Nugent insisted on doing everything by the book.

"I felt sorry for him," says Lewis. "He'd learned the hard way that the police department is a fraternal organization only in the best of times. When you fuck up, you fuck up on your own. He wanted to be a cop because he thought cops could do a lot of good. Well, a cop can help little kids across the street, but that's about it."

In Lewis' view, it was Nugent's desire to be a hero that had gotten him into trouble. He told Lewis he was ringing off duty one night at the corner of Hollis and Pond in South Weymouth, a desolate spot by a boarded-up train station and battered American Legion post, when a white Thunderbird went screeching past. A more experienced cop would probably have let the incident pass, but Nugent, fresh out of the police academy, was bent on bringing the driver to justice. Since there weren't enough squad cars to go around, Nugent had to give chase in his own car, a green Pontiac convertible. He shined a flashlight on himself when he caught up with the Thunderbird to let the speedster know he was tangling with the law. The driver, one Tommy O'Brien, responded by trying to knock Nugent's car into a tree as he pulled abreast, and Nugent decided to arrest him for felonious assault.

He fired three warning shots out the window, but O'Brien kept going.

The two cars whizzed through Weymouth at speeds of up to eighty miles an hour for over four miles before the Thunderbird took a sharp left into a dead-end street and pulled up at a shabby wooden bungalow, where O'Brien sprinted for the door. Nugent was convinced the kid was running in to take hostages, although it was in fact the boy's mother's house. Nugent scrambled after him with his gun drawn. Just inside the door, O'Brien grabbed for the revolver. There was a struggle, then an explosion, and Tommy O'Brien lay dead with a bullet in his temple.

Nugent's report described the fatal shooting as an accident caused by the recklessness of the deceased.

O'Brien's mother had emerged from the living room at the first sounds of the scuffle and she told a different story. She said that Nugent had yelled at her to call the police, but while she was on the phone, she'd distinctly heard the cop scream at her son, "You were speeding, you bastard, and now I'm going to kill you!" before the fatal shot rang out. She'd turned from the phone to see her son lying in a pool of blood.

The judge at the probable-cause hearing believed her. Presiding at Quincy Courthouse, the scene of Lewis' earlier encounter with the masked intruders, Judge Paul Connolly listened to three days of arguments and concluded that he didn't think O'Brien had committed "felonious assault" with his reckless driving, nor, even, that Nugent had had any right to follow O'Brien into the house to arrest him. "Therefore," the judge decided, "I can reasonably conclude that the defendant, Officer Nugent, is guilty of probable cause to manslaughter." He would have to be tried.

Standing next to Lewis, the rookie patrolman paled, and his knees buckled. Lewis grabbed him by the jacket, but the cloth ripped away and Nugent dropped like a load of bricks onto the floor.

Late into the night Lewis pondered the situation and concluded that the key to the case was the four-mile chase from the South Weymouth intersection to the O'Briens' bungalow. If he could prove O'Brien really had tried to knock Nugent off the road during the chase, it would justify Nugent's following him in through the door with his gun drawn and it would make the officer's version of the scuffle far more believable.

To check out Nugent's story, Lewis revved up his own doddering Le Sabre one night and sped down the route. Yes, the whole thing was all quite possible. Scary as hell, but possible. Lewis turned up some skid marks and a roughed-up patch of grass near a tree Nugent had almost hit after O'Brien knocked into him. Using a trick from his adjusting work, Lewis compared the dents on the right front of Nugent's Pontiac and the left front of O'Brien's Thunderbird. They meshed pretty well, but unfortunately, no paint—the best evidence of a collision—had been transferred from one to the other. The matching indentations constituted only circumstantial evidence. To win Nugent's case, Lewis would need witnesses.

Lewis says he must have pounded on a hundred doors along the four-mile stretch on Main and Front streets that summer, asking if anyone had heard any honking, squealing of tires, or shots on July 8. Most of the people he asked were bored by the question, saying they heard as much *every* night as teen-agers whooped it up along the strip. Some, angry that Lewis would defend a killer cop, turned hostile. One elderly gentleman—"the last of the starched-collar set," says Lewis—told the detective: "I hope they *hang* Wayne Nugent along with every cop in this country. And"—he looked Lewis in the eye—"may I add every investigator."

The best Lewis could do was turn up a woman who said that just after she'd turned on Johnny Carson, she did hear some "firecrackers," followed by such a screech of tires she was afraid a car

53

was going to tip over. But she hadn't bothered to go to the window to take a look.

Desperate for witnesses, Lewis drove the route himself a month of Saturdays in hopes of turning up a salesman, factory worker, a waitress—anyone whose weekly schedule might have brought him through the area on the Saturday night of the shooting. He jotted down twenty license-plate numbers, secured the names of the drivers from the registry, and called them all. A huge effort; nothing came of it.

And the harder it became to prove that O'Brien actually had resisted arrest so violently, the more likely it seemed to Lewis that he was the sort who would have. Checking police files and interviewing acquaintances (O'Brien seemed not to have any real friends), he found out that O'Brien had a penchant for high speeds and violence. What was more, Lewis discovered that O'Brien had just come from a bar when he roared through Nugent's intersection, and the bartender admitted that O'Brien had left the place "pretty wobbly." But to his frustration, Lewis couldn't introduce any of this evidence, since Nugent couldn't have known it at the time.

At the very least, Lewis had to refute what O'Brien's mother was

saying or, as he says, "Nugent was done." He contacted the operator who had handled Mrs. O'Brien's call to the police. Maybe the operator had overheard Nugent's supposed outburst? Better yet, maybe she hadn't.

He learned that she had indeed been on the line when the shot was fired. The sound had almost blown out her eardrum! And no, she hadn't heard any "I'm going to kill you."

After nearly three solid months of work, it was the best evidence Lewis had. He was beginning to wonder a little about his client. He didn't doubt that O'Brien had jostled Nugent on the four-mile chase, but he questioned whether Nugent had been able to hold his temper once he had drawn his gun and O'Brien stood defenseless before him. Lewis had trouble containing his own anger from time to time, and he knew it was a standard line for cops to plead self-defense after they'd killed a suspect. If Nugent was impulsive enough to have gone chasing after a speedster in his own car in the first place, who knew what he'd do? Lewis felt that he had drawn the losing side on his first big case.

Because of the anti-police sentiment sweeping the country, Bellotti recommended waiving Nugent's right to a jury trial and letting his fate be decided solely by Judge Tomasello in District Court. Local press attention had waned over the summer and now, in early October, the courtroom was filled mostly with off-duty policemen. The prosecution, led by District Attorney George Burke, started with the Medical Examiner's recitation of the cause of death and ended four days later with its ace witness, the robust Mrs. O'Brien, who repeated her story that the policeman had called her son a "bastard" and then shot him for speeding.

About midnight that night, at the Hancock Street offices, Lewis and Bellotti were glumly looking for holes in the prosecution's case and plotting the presentation of their currently none-too-seaworthy defense when the phone rang. It was a Mrs. Pinsky, who announced that she had read Mrs. O'Brien's testimony in the evening papers and was sure the woman was lying.

Mildly incredulous, Lewis asked her to explain.

"Well," continued Mrs. Pinsky, "on the morning of the shooting I met Mrs. O'Brien at the Weymouth bus stop. We got talking, and she said she was going to Community Opticians in Quincy to get her hearing aid fixed. Hers was giving her this terrible buzzing. She told me she was very upset about it because she'd already taken in her spare one and she can't hear a thing without it. Absolutely stone deaf."

Lewis dialed the Quincy police, knowing they keep a list of home numbers of all the town's shop owners in case of a break-in or a fire after hours. He reached the Quincy Community Opticians manager, George Nash, at one-thirty that morning at his Weymouth home. Nash was not pleased to be called at that hour, but when Lewis explained that the life of a patrolman was at stake, he softened up and told the detective to meet him at his Quincy shop in half an hour. There he went through his records and discovered that Mrs. Pinsky was right—both of Mrs. O'Brien's hearing aids had been in for repairs the night of the murder. She couldn't have heard a word, not even from the operator. Nash agreed to take the stand the next morning to repeat to the court what he'd just told the investigator.

Bellotti was cagey in cross-examining Mrs. O'Brien. He asked her to repeat exactly what she'd heard the patrolman yell before the gun went off. " 'You were speeding, you bastard, and now I'm going to kill you,' " Mrs. O'Brien said, carefully enunciating each word. Bellotti asked her to say it again—he hadn't quite caught all of it. . . . The woman ran through it again, every word.

Bellotti asked her how her hearing was.

"Fine," said Mrs. O'Brien. "I have a hearing aid now, but with it I hear perfectly."

"And you had it in on the night of the shooting, of course," continued Bellotti sweetly.

"Oh, yes, of course," said Mrs. O'Brien.

Bellotti sent an aide to fetch Mr. Nash, who had been waiting outside the courthouse. Nash testified that on the night in question the hearing aid was not in Mrs. O'Brien's ear but in his office, and he produced the records to prove it. The courtroom rustled at the news. Wayne Nugent was called to the stand to give his version of the events one more time, but before he finished, Judge Tomasello dismissed him. "I feel there is not sufficient evidence to find this man guilty," he announced, and marched abruptly out of the courtroom.

Lewis' career soared after that. Bellotti even broke his no-compliment rule to tell everybody that Gil had been the whole case and the defense would have died without him. Detective work came piling in for Lewis from attorneys all over the state, and he was able to move at last out of his matchbox Norwell home into the spacious house he still owns on a hill in Wollaston. The new place was so big, there was even room for his office. At the age of thirty-five, he finally had his show on the road.

"At night nothing comes between you and your subject. No massive traffic jams to get in the way. And the cops are all in the doughnut shops."

FIVE

Midnight Rider

The easiest time for Lewis to tail someone is at night. His car, when seen in his subject's rearview mirror, is just another pair of luminous headlights. The subject's car, however, is another matter. While headlights are fairly uniform, taillights are almost all different: some narrow vertical slits, some circles, some horizontal stripes—all easily distinguishable.

The taillights of Irving Feldman's Thunderbird were a thick band of red light that stretched clear across the car's posterior; and the directional signal was even more eye-catching, firing its segments sequentially like, says Lewis, "the swishing of a tiger's tail."

A balding lawyer and marriage counselor, Feldman appeared to have shifted his relationship with one of his clients, Lois Higgins, to a more personal level, much to the distress of Lois' husband. Raymond Higgins had begun to suspect something was amiss after Feldman switched the couple's joint counseling sessions to individual ones during the hour. Higgins began to realize that he was receiving considerably less than thirty minutes each time, and his wife considerably more. More alarming, as the duration of her visits increased, the length of her skirts shortened, and the fabric was often rumpled and her lipstick smudged when she finally emerged. Finally, Higgins could contain his suspicions no longer, and one day he removed his shoes, tiptoed down the hallway to Feldman's office, and pressed his ear against the door. He listened for thirty seconds and didn't hear a word. What kind of therapy was this?

When Mrs. Higgins filed for divorce a month later, she began to work as Feldman's secretary. On the advice of his attorney, Higgins turned to Gil Lewis.

Lewis knew Feldman would be elusive, since, as a lawyer and a counselor, he had everything to lose if word leaked out about an affair with a client. "The news would blow his ticket forever," says the detective. Sure enough, Feldman confined his socializing with his new secretary to the interior of his Thunderbird. And to make extra sure they avoided any observers, he stayed on the go, and performed such fancy maneuvers as running several times around all rotaries, making sudden U-turns on highways, jumping lanes at every opportunity, and pulling abruptly into highway breakdown lanes.

Feldman was prepared for everything except Gil Lewis.

Lewis had no trouble sticking on him. The detective hung back three hundred yards and stayed in the right lane, from where, if Feldman turned off, that glowing tiger's-tail directional signal would have to cross Lewis' sight line. When Feldman pulled up suddenly and Lewis went sailing past, Gil just waited up ahead at a bend in the road, careful to glide to a stop lest his own taillights flare when he hit his brakes. On rotaries, Lewis merely turned off and watched in his rearview mirror which way Feldman went, then doubled back to follow him. If Feldman chose the same turn-off Lewis had taken, so much the better. Lewis kept going. People suspecting a tail never guess they're actually being led.

And with such techniques, it wasn't long before Lewis got this evidence, although it meant staying with the couple one night for two hundred and fifty miles. Lewis tailed them through two neighboring states before they finally dropped back down to a little Massachusetts town, pulled into the parking lot of a late-night bar called the Blue Tiara, and fell into each other's arms.

Lewis looped around to enter the bar's parking lot the back way. He lined up his Instamatic so that the shot would include the Blue

Tiara's blazing neon sign, the couple in the Thunderbird, and the license plates of the cars on either side for further verification, and clicked.

—

"NOT THE BIGGEST BUT THE BEST," reads Lewis' ad in the Quincy Yellow Pages. "SURVEILLANCE OUR SPECIALTY." While Lewis takes pride in all aspects of his work, his surveillance techniques are the ones that truly set him apart. Whether it means sticking with subjects for hours on the highway or in the maze of one-way streets downtown or watching a window all night from his parked car, Lewis does the job. On a typical night he usually drives three hundred miles, most of them in circles as he checks on the various domestic cases—often as many as four or five—he has going at any one time.

Lewis tracks missing persons mostly by phone and performs defense interviews in person, but he investigates adultery cases from his car: tailing romantic wanderers like Feldman on their nocturnal trysts, parking by bedroom windows to catch a glimpse of clandestine lovers through the curtains, cruising through apartment parking lots in search of a certain straying husband's automobile. Lewis does not actually have to catch anyone in the act of

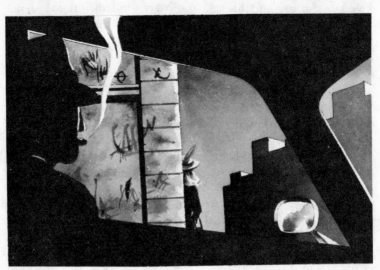

extramarital sex (nor does he wish to); he just has to establish, as he says, "inclination and opportunity" in order to give his client more leverage in a divorce settlement. Despite the sexual revolution, judges in Massachusetts still take a dim view of adultery, and if it appears that the affair has led to the dissolution of the marriage, they come down hard on the offender, raising alimony payments, reducing child visitation, and seizing property.

Since Lewis spends as much as fifteen hours a day in his car, he inevitably develops a certain fondness for it. "My car's my house," he says. He even outfitted one surveillance van with chairs and a desk to make it into a portable living room.

Lewis now drives a powerful Toyota Supra hatchback that has all the extras, and stocks it with a stash of Muriel Coronella packets and Go Ahead candy bars. The back seat is covered with a heap of newspapers, some out-of-state maps, a couple of sweaters, a raincoat, and his BMW baseball cap. No one ever rides back there.

The Supra is an extremely comfortable second home, yet from the outside it is just another average-looking, fuel-efficient economy car. "My cars are all like me," says Lewis. "They look harmless, but they have a lot of power in reserve." To make sure the car doesn't stand out, Lewis removed the dealer's eye-catching reflective red emblem and painted the car gray—the color that he's settled on, after a period of favoring dark blue, as the one least distinguishable at night. He's kept the car free of dents, decals, and bumper stickers. And he changes the license plate every six months. The vehicle is now, like the driver, perfectly nondescript.

And inside the car, it's always dark and smoky. Lewis insists on having heavily tinted windows and dark upholstery, and he unscrews the light bulb overhead to keep from illuminating himself at night when he opens the car door. He has even removed the tiny lights on the instrument panel under the dashboard. But he leaves the light on the radio, since he almost never plays it.

People rarely notice him as he sits inside, waiting and watching. Pedestrians sometimes pound on the roof and kick the tires thinking the car is empty. And as an unseen watcher, Lewis is witness to the strangest things, quite apart from the escapades of his adulterers. Parked by an ice cream parlor not long ago, he watched a carload of kids pull up beside a Volkswagen, haul out its passengers, and start brawling. Moments later, an Oldsmobile stopped at a red light on the street, and a woman burst out of the car and ran to the far side of the ice cream store. When the driver chased after her, the woman dashed around the building back to the car and drove off, leaving her companion screaming on the sidewalk.

Lewis just watched. The only time he's ever interfered with this kind of activity was to call the police one night when he saw a man climb the pilings on the waterfront in an apparent suicide attempt.

"At night," says Lewis, "everything's in black and white, like a forties movie. I like it. Color's a distraction. The night seems to me to be more factual, more real." And his eyes are accustomed to it. While his own Supra blends into the dark, he never misses a suspect's car. "I don't see detail," he says, "just the general outline of the car and the plate number. I don't know how, but I always get a clear picture of the car in my mind. And when I see it again, I always know." Indeed, he remembers cars vividly for years, long after he's moved onto other cases and other plate numbers. He rarely passes a night on the city streets without spotting a car that brings back old memories.

He has little trouble, too, identifying people in the dark. "It's easier without color," he says. "Color changes. Color of garments, color of hair, color of skin—tans, redness—all change. The night gives me what I need, which is shape and movement. I go by the slope of the shoulders, the way the clothing is worn, the gait. These never change."

Most years Lewis runs up sixty thousand miles on his odometer, most of it on these nocturnal surveillances. He has, however, put in as much as twenty thousand miles on a single case. His nightly territory can take in all of eastern Massachusetts, and sometimes most of New England. Nevertheless, Lewis rarely uses maps. He says they confuse him.

Instead, he relies on his own internal compass (supplemented by the knowledge that odd-numbered interstate highways run north–south, even ones east–west) and occasional instructions from local gas-attendants to get him where he's going.

He always feels at home out there. "I love driving at night," he says, "always have. I used to take long midnight rides when I was a kid. Sixteen, seventeen, I used to love driving around. I had a 1941 Buick that I bought from my brother Leon when he went into the

Army. It was a big, four-door Roadmaster covered with chrome and had an eight-cylinder engine and those rough velvet seats, arm cushions, four cigarette lighters, and under-the-seat heaters. My friend Paul Higgins and I would ride around in it all night long. He was a midnight rider too. We'd go to Providence for coffee, or down to Times Square in New York for pizza, or to Cape Cod to walk the beaches. It was great.

"I like the city at night. I like any place at night because it's so much calmer and there are no bright colors to distract you. It's like riding a bike on Sunday afternoon. You can see everything. You're the sole observer.

"There are so few people around—that's the best thing. That's beautiful. I don't like to be in crowds, or to observe them. When you're the only one up, it's your city, so the things you want to look at you can take the time to see. You can place things in your mind better at night. I have a tendency to squint, and that brightness really hurts my eyes. At night, nothing comes between you and your subject. No massive traffic jams to get in the way. And the cops are all in the doughnut shops.

"The best part of the night is between eleven-thirty and two-thirty in the morning, when the show crowds and the drunks have gone home. You have the streets to yourself, and if you know where the people are—there's a drugstore at the Charles Street Circle that's all hustle and bustle—you can avoid them. And along Memorial Drive at night there's a beautiful view of the river. Sometimes I'll park there, get out of my car, and stand along the railing and enjoy the city. I also like Copley Square. The street musicians stay out late there during the summer. Sometimes I reminisce a little and drive by Park Square, where I worked at the Greyhound Bus Terminal. I used to enjoy cruising Mass. Ave. down by the nightclub the Big M, but that's torn down now. I'd get out and watch the hookers. It was really something to see all the respectable middle- and upper-class businessmen turn into night prowlers and go down there adventuring for whores.

"There isn't much out in the suburbs at night, though. Sometimes I'll take a ride up to the top of the hill at Point Allerton in Hull where there's an old World War Two gun emplacement in a little park. You can see the Boston skyline from there."

Lewis has gone through twelve cars in the last five years, most of them obtained through For Sale ads in local papers of the wealthier suburbs. That way he buys reasonably priced cars in good condition.

"The key words for my cars are 'functional' and 'unobtrusive,' " he says. "One detective I know, Billy, always drives a beat-up old wreck, and he almost got his head blown off once because of it. He parked outside a witness' house one night and went up to the door to interview the guy, but got no answer. Billy found out later the guy was home, all right—waiting behind his door with a shotgun. He saw Billy's car and figured it was a burglar.

"So I drive a decent, average car, one that starts quietly. And I always wait for another car to approach before I hit the engine, to mask the sound. On hills, I park heading down the incline so I can coast out of earshot before turning the switch. My car has to have a good muffler, too, to run quietly and to protect me from carbon monoxide poisoning on long idles. And the seats have to be comfortable, easy on the backside." As it is, Lewis does all his early-morning weight lifting largely to restore the muscle tone he has lost behind the wheel the night before.

But most of all, Lewis' cars have to be powerful. He recalls fondly the days before mileage standards and pollution control. "The '66 Buick and the '69 Le Sabre, they had big, ballsy engines, 350 cc's," he says. "Those babies could *fly*! It's a good feeling to have that power behind you when you need it. The best, though, is to be driving a raggedy-looking shitbox with a good engine that can keep up with the best-looking brand-new one. You may look like the underdog, but down deep you know you're not."

Lewis was tailing an ex–football star once when the subject suddenly shot ahead on Route 95. Unfortunately, Lewis was driving his wife's old car, and he was somewhat unnerved as he mashed down the accelerator and saw the speedometer climb to the top of the gauge, a hundred miles an hour, and strain to go further. "I get frightened at high speeds," admits the detective—who, nonetheless, never wears a seat belt. "The guy must have been doing at least one-ten, and Nancy's car was shivering and shaking all over the place. And I've done enough insurance work to know that at that speed it doesn't take much to total a car. But I stuck with him for a hundred miles clear to Portland. Otherwise I'd have had to do it all over again. I guess that was my speed record."

His mark for endurance he established over four days in 1970 when he followed a North Shore horse fancier, with two steeds in tow, from Boston all the way to Chicago. En route, Lewis procured considerable evidence of the man's liberated attitude toward marriage, watching with interest as the equestrian picked up a new lady for each leg of the journey—Boston–New York, New York–Cleveland, Cleveland–Toledo, and Toledo–Chicago.

Of course, much of the time Lewis spends on surveillance he's not moving at all. In fact, he often parks so long in one place that he has to allay the suspicions of meter maids by giving them boxes of candy and explaining quietly that he's waiting to visit his wife, who's sick with cancer at a nearby hospital. In the suburbs he makes a point of parking on the street between two houses, so residents of each will assume the man in the strange car is waiting for their neighbor.

Slumped down in his seat, so that viewed from the front or back the outline of his body is concealed by the headrest, with his BMW cap pulled down low over his eyes, Lewis goes about his solitary business. "I learned that from Roger," he says. "You should see him on surveillance. He's incredible. He pulls his hat down over his eyes like me, but he gets down so low in this seat, he's practically gone, like an alligator watching from a swamp.

"I never get drowsy," Lewis says. "Out on surveillance I establish a mind-set where it's me against them. If the guy I'm following is smarter than I am, then shame on me; but I've never trailed anybody yet who was. I think how much of an asshole I'd be if I let him beat me because my concentration lapsed. So I try to focus all my senses on the surveillance. I think of different ways to position the vehicle—on a tight dead-end street, say; or I might remember how one guy got away from me fifteen, twenty years ago on this kind of case. I try never to make the same mistake twice, by thinking of all possible ways that guy can beat me. I *never* let him beat me. Also, I set up the best time to cruise, I make observations of everything in the neighborhood to see if anybody is watching me, and I pick up the pattern of when police come by in their cruisers. I may daydream, but it's always a constructive daydream where I wonder about the characters in the case I'm working on, because every client I've ever met is a story to me. I think about how people can really fuck up their lives for instant gratification."

Already a master of delaying his own gratification, Lewis once considered enrolling in a Silva Mind Control seminar to improve his concentration, but quit when he discovered that his powers already exceeded those of his instructors. "It's mind over matter," he says. "I see myself as someone who can always control the needs and impulses of the body." Even Boston's extreme temperatures fail to bend his resolve, although some days he'll have to drink a case of Pepsi because of the heat. He says he has developed a "leather bladder" as well.

The cold, however, can be even worse, since Lewis is reluctant to start his engine to activate the heat. But for the most part, he views the cold as a blessing, because the snow makes it easier to gauge how long a subject's car has been in position, or when it left.

Lewis likes a fair fight, so he avoids the special advantages that would make his task simpler. While he acknowledges that the best method for tailing someone would be to use two or three cars operating in radio communication, he doesn't bother with it. Not only would it be too expensive: it would rob him of the challenge. "I use the same car night after night," he says, "to make sure I can stay invisible. Besides, I don't take shortcuts."

When he needs to throw his subjects off, he resorts to more ingenious techniques. He'll hop on his motorcycle, or pedal a tenspeed, or lace up his sneakers to jog, or before he gave his dog away, he'd walk Mr. Moto through on a leash. The cycling enthusiasm has, however, faded somewhat since he had to ditch a $200 Motobecane in the New Hampshire woods for a quick getaway when someone called the police on him.

But for really sticky surveillances, Lewis rolls out his "Bell Telephone" van. The idea came to him during a watch on a lanky engineer who was carrying on an extramarital affair after hours in his office in a South Shore industrial park. Since the place was buzzing with security patrol cars, the detective couldn't get close enough to the building. But he noticed that Bell Tel vans, busy installing new phones, could park right by the front door. So Lewis invested in a van and drove it to a friendly garage for a custom paint job— cream on top, pale green on the bottom and the familiar Bell emblem on either side. The detective had only to inform the mechanics that the van was a "surveillance unit" to get the job done with no further questions. He nuzzled the restyled minibus in with all the other Bell vans by the office building a few nights later. "Nobody gave me a second look," Lewis says proudly. Including the engineer and his lady friend, whom Lewis photographed with ease from the van windows as they walked in and out the front door arm in arm.

Lewis takes pride in his track record. Other investigators have been known to blow cases when they've taken battery-powered TV sets along for entertainment on surveillance, or when they've rear-ended their subjects on the highway. Lewis, by contrast, has been "made," as he calls it, only twice, and both times it happened because his clients had tipped their spouses off. About half his clients are unable to resist needling their mates with the information Lewis has turned up. Hints like these, obviously, made Lewis' career tougher. One almost ended it.

Lewis had pursued a local plumber over most of the sprawling South Shore one night, along beach roads and up inland side streets before seeing him turn into a narrow dirt road. Lewis says he has a sixth sense that alerts him to impending danger, and he felt decidedly apprehensive as he plunged down this winding two-track path. Lewis' car scraped against the scraggly bushes on either side that stood out starkly in his headlights. Otherwise everything was carbon black, and quiet, too, except for the sea thrashing in the distance.

Then suddenly, in a blur to his right, somebody burst out at him from the bushes. It was the plumber, wearing a tattered white T-shirt that glowed eerily in the bright light. His eyes shone as he shrieked "I'm gonna kill you!" and smashed the hood of Lewis' car with a baseball bat. A second blow knocked off Lewis' antenna. But by then Lewis had jammed his car into reverse, and the wheels kicked up a spray of dust as he shot backward out of the lane. When he reached home, Nancy was sobbing hysterically. The plumber's wife, Lewis' client, had called to say her husband had killed the investigator and left him in a ditch.

But Lewis is used to sudden appearances. A face in the window, a man at the door, a car in the drive, all of them set his cylinders rotating. At such times, his heartbeat doesn't jump, or his breathing accelerate. His body just seems to burn a higher, purer octane.

His movements are powerful, yet precise. He's ready to leap into silent pursuit, or quick evasive action—whatever the situation requires. Whether it is the raising of a shade or the lowering of a gun, to Lewis it's all the same. It's *action*.

"That's what I live for," he says.

"I'm the last of a vanishing breed."

SIX

Private Investigator, Private Citizen

"People sometimes ask me if I mind spending so much time alone," Lewis says. "But really, what's there to mind?" To the detective, the solitary life is the beauty of his job. It gives him the same feeling of liberation that he found atop those teetering radar poles in the military. Perilous at times, but exhilarating. He doesn't have to take orders, or give any either—except possibly to Roger Grove. "But I'm long past worrying about Roger," he says. And his freedom allows him to concentrate all his energy on the task at hand, whether it's shadowing a wandering wife, tracking a missing person, or probing a murder. "I control the whole thing top to bottom," he says. "I'm my own man."

His life seems to epitomize the myth of the private eye, slipping quietly and alone through treacherous streets and alleys. Yet Lewis recognizes that the truth is somewhat more complicated. At his little agency, Lewis may be independent, but by no means is he totally free. Even the detective business has strict rules, and Lewis has learned to play by them.

To begin with, there's that eight-by-ten investigator's license on his wall. It's issued by the state Department of Public Safety, in accordance with six pages in the statute book, to those who meet the

69

state's stringent requirements: three year's experience, three impressive references, the posting of a $5,000 bond, and payment of a $750 fee ($400 yearly to renew). With this license, a private investigator is allowed to conduct the criminal-defense investigations and missing-persons searches, domestic surveillances and background checks.

A private investigator is subject to all the regulations that govern the private citizen. In fact, the statute even tacks on a few more: It forbids him from taking part in labor disputes—a curious holdover from the strikebreaking practices of the Pinkerton Detectives at the turn of the century. It requires him to keep the information he uncovers confidential, to be revealed only in court. Like any private citizen, he must not impersonate a police officer. And to make sure the detective obeys all these regulations, he is subject to a yearly review. "I have to pay one of the highest license fees in the country," Lewis grouses, "but I don't get anything for it except a piece of paper."

Nevertheless, Lewis takes that piece of paper very seriously. It's his only master. "I think about it all the time," he says. "It's the only thing that keeps me in business. I'm constantly aware of all the things I can't do out on the job. I can't invade anybody's privacy, or tap a phone. Even if it didn't cost me my job, it would certainly blow my case in court. That's the first thing attorneys think of when they hear a private investigator's been on the case— they try to get his evidence thrown out on privacy grounds. So I never take those kinds of shortcuts. I never break into somebody's house, or even cross their property unless I'm invited. But clients never understand that. They think I have special license to break the law. They're always asking me to do a black-bag job or tap a phone. Some clients even want me to crack a guy's legs or knock him off. What do they take me for? My answer is always the same: I'm not going to the can for anybody, especially *you*."

An opposing lawyer on a divorce case once found this out when he tried to coax some information out of Lewis about his client over breakfast at a pancake house. Compelled by statute to keep information about his clients confidential, Lewis wasn't about to say anything. He became suspicious when the lawyer lifted his briefcase up onto the table and seemed to point it toward the investigator. Lewis could see tiny holes drilled through the leather.

To the lawyer's surprise, Lewis reached out and popped the case open to expose a little tape recorder humming quietly inside.

"Hey—now, Gil—really, I didn't know it was on," sputtered the attorney.

Lewis didn't comment. He plucked the recorder out, threw it on the floor, stomped on it with his boots, and dropped the crumpled remains back on the table. "Don't you ever try that again," he snapped, and stalked out.

———

Lewis is no less conscious of the laws of economics, and lately the small detective agency has been going the way of the independent gas station and the neighborhood butcher shop.

"I'm the last of a vanishing breed," he says. "Back in the forties there were lots of small agencies like mine getting by on the divorce work and criminal investigations. There was plenty of work to go around. That was the golden age. Now—well, it's tough."

Many of the investigators who go under have only themselves to blame. Lewis was once called in for consultation by a pair of former prison officials who six months previously had tried to launch new careers as private detectives. They had mortgaged their homes to lease a fancy downtown office, hire a curvaceous secretary, and purchase nickel-plated automatics (for that "Hi-yo, Silver!" look). Now they wanted to know why they had no clients.

"I asked them what kind of advertising they used," Lewis recalls. "They looked at me kind of funny. Advertising? It had never *occurred* to them. They went bankrupt a little while later. I found out because one of them called me about a job."

Lewis himself relies on his little ad in the Yellow Pages, whatever publicity might swing his way from a headline case, and a solid reputation in the city's legal community to bring in his customers. One of the job's peculiarities, however, is that no matter how skillfully he might perform those lucrative domestic cases, he never gets a customer through word of mouth. "Nobody's ever going to stand up at a party and say they've had their husband followed by Gil Lewis," he explains. "Once you do the work on those cases, you die." Mindful of his delicate finances, he keeps his office in his house and sticks to those secondhand cars. And for the same reason, Lewis pays close attention to his rates.

"There's an art to figuring out how much to charge," he says.

"You've got to strike the right balance between money up front and the dough you get after you've produced some results. Ask for too much up front and you scare the client off. Too little and you get burned. It's true that I've been known to take a case for nothing, but I always think of it as a chance to sharpen my skills, so there's some profit in it for me.

"But Roger's terrible at the money end of the business, and that's why he's still working for me after all these years. He does great investigation, but I'm the one who always has to set the cases up. If I'd left that to Roger, I would have been out of business years ago."

Indeed, Lewis can recall long stretches earlier in his career when business was so slow, he passed weeks at a time walking Wollaston Beach. "I'd change my shirt several times a day," he says, "so that I'd feel like I was working."

Those were the days when the changing social climate was shifting the demand for detective work away from the single operator. "Times have changed since the forties," Lewis explains. "Divorce isn't the big thing it used to be back then. There isn't that much money in it for a detective anymore. Nowadays the big money is in security work, because everybody's so scared about being ripped off. Retailers and wholesalers are clamoring for protection. Security is now a multibillion-dollar industry. Divorces can't compete with it. So that's what most detectives have shifted over to. But you can't do it with a little agency. You've got to be big, the bigger the better. The owners want bodies out there protecting their stuff. *Lots* of bodies. So look in the Yellow Pages under DETECTIVES and all you'll see is SECURITY, SECURITY, SECURITY. The only one who doesn't do that stuff is me.

"I knew from the start I could never get into that security stuff. I also knew that if I just stuck to one thing, the pure investigation, eventually I'd get to be the best at it and people would have to come to me. In this business, you see, there are artists and there are businessmen, and I'm an artist."

Fortunately for Lewis, art sells. "Clients know that at my agency they get me and only me," he says, "and I'm accountable. I'm involved in all the cases Roger works on too, so even though he's like my right arm, the clients still get Gil Lewis." Clients can feel assured that Lewis, as both owner and operator, has a financial stake in the success of their investigation. They must also appreciate the personal touch that comes with the small scale. They don't have to worry that their case will be caught up in the communications problems and petty jealousies that can crop up in a more bureaucratic outfit. They can be assured that the sensitive but time-consuming surveillances will be done by Lewis, and not farmed out to a $5-an-hour operative as happens at the larger agencies. And Lewis can boast not only twenty years' experience in the field, but also the wide range of talents, from his tracking skills to his knowledge of legal procedure, that comes from handling personally all the cases in his highly varied business.

Others might worry that this little agency would fall between the cracks of the larger investigative outfits, but Lewis knows better. He is not in the least threatened by the likes of the FBI, the police, the insurance investigators, the security firms, Pinkerton's; Lewis, with his one part-time associate, one car, and office in his living room, knows he can compete with the best. He doesn't even own a proper I.D. card to show who, and what, he is. His Lewis Detective Agency business card lists only his name, his phone number, and the word "LICENSED" in the upper right-hand corner. He relies on his manner to dispel any doubts about his authority. He likes the low profile: it highlights his skills.

Lewis gives the police as a point of comparison. For all their resources, Lewis knows they make mistakes. "Sure cops have power," he says, "they may have the badge and the stick and the blue suit; but I think the power I have makes me much more effective. The cops have this institutional mentality. They think they can bull their way through anything. I know how to work my way around things to get what I need. Cops are so aggressive, so overt. They always assume that if somebody tries to stop them, they can just flash a badge. Well, it doesn't always work. If they go to someone's house to take a statement and the guy says no, they demand it, threatening to drag him down to the station, or telling him he'd better call his lawyer. But that just makes the guy dig in his heels all the more. What you need in this business is what I've got: persistence and charm."

Lewis has survived on his finely developed craft. His customers have found out that while he may cost a little more and occasionally take a little longer, he consistently provides quality work and personal service. And in a business like Lewis', that is important. A life may depend on it. Hillary Bingham's did.

————

Something of a free spirit, twenty-seven-year-old Hillary Bingham lived alone on the "wrong" side of Beacon Hill, despite a host of suitors and a large inheritance. She worked in a downtown ad agency and played ferocious tennis. "She was built like a racehorse," says Lewis admiringly, "just a wholesome, lovely-looking broad."

One summer evening, Bingham returned from a tennis game to her tiny apartment, crammed with modern art and Victorian antiques, around ten o'clock, took a shower, and went to bed. Because of the heat, she lay naked on top of the sheet on her rickety brass bed. It didn't trouble her that she had no shades on her bedroom windows, or that there was a fire escape running down four flights to the narrow street right outside. Around two, she woke up feeling thirsty and walked sleepily to the refrigerator to drink some juice, then went back to bed.

She woke sometime later with a knife at her throat. "Don't scream," said a male voice, "or I'll kill you." As her eyes adjusted

to the half-light she could just make out a thin man with jet-black hair, tattoos on his bare arms, and a horrifying scar that ran across his forehead and curved down to his nose. "Why didn't you give me a drink?" he said. "I was sitting right there in the kitchen when you came in. Why didn't you offer me some?"

"I-I d-didn't know you were there," Bingham answered haltingly, terrified to think she'd been watched the whole time.

She made a move to cover herself with the sheet, but the man pressed more firmly on the knife at her throat. With his free hand he pushed the hair back from her forehead as if to get a better look at her; then he ran his hand across her cheek and down over her breasts. As he touched her, he watched her eyes to gauge her reaction. But she showed none. Her whole body was stiff with fear.

He told her how beautiful she was, and then he slid down beside her on the bed and raped her. He did it over and over, in a variety of ways, all of them painful and humiliating. Between assaults he asked her to sit and talk with him over a cup of coffee in the kitchen. She could barely speak, but she knew her life depended on cooperating, so she complied with everything the man asked. Then he pushed her back to the bed and started all over.

Finally, at about seven the next morning, he was done with her. But before he left he searched her apartment and pocketed her money and address book. He told Hillary that if she went to the police, he'd kill her family—he could see from the book that they all lived in the area—starting with her sister. He also jotted down her home and work telephone numbers and told her he'd be in touch.

"Maybe we can do this again sometime," he said.

When he was gone, Bingham cried for an hour. Then she took a shower and went out for a long walk. Afterward she couldn't remember what streets she'd taken, but she ended up that afternoon at the police station, where she found herself telling everything to a lieutenant in the criminal division.

Clearheaded now, Bingham was able to give the police a good description of her attacker. After sending her to the lab to test her for traces of semen that would corroborate her tale, the police told her their plan. Since the rapist had taken Bingham's phone numbers and hinted he might return, they wanted to lay a trap for him, with Bingham as the bait. When the lieutenant assured her that he'd put the department's top detectives on the case, Bingham agreed to cooperate. But she was still scared, for herself and for her family.

On a steamy afternoon the following week, Bingham got a call at work. "Hello, Hillary," said a voice. "It's me." She knew who "me" was. Sticking to the plan, she told him how much she'd enjoyed making love with him that night and—she bit her lip—she'd like him to come back. The caller paused a moment to think, then said he'd be there next Saturday night.

The police were gratified by the news and promised to have a four-man undercover team in position outside her apartment around the clock until her attacker showed up. Still, just to feel safe, Hillary explained the situation to a girlfriend and persuaded her to stay over that Saturday.

Bingham grew increasingly nervous as the hour of her "date" approached. She couldn't bring herself to eat and couldn't concentrate on the card games her friend wanted to play to pass the time. Finally, around ten-thirty, there was a loud knock at the door. Certain it was the police coming to say her troubles were over, she pulled back the bolt and swung the door open.

It wasn't the police. It was the thin man with the horrible scar. He jumped inside and came straight for Hillary. She screamed, and the girlfriend charged at him from the sofa. Together, they managed to push him back out the door, beating on him with their fists. The two heard him flee down the stairs. From the window they watched him dash off down the street.

Trembling, Hillary dialed police headquarters, but the lieutenant handling her case was off duty and no one else knew much about it. They offered to send out a cruiser, but Hillary declined. She'd lost all faith in the police. She left her apartment to spend the weekend at her friend's house. On Monday she called the lieutenant in a fury. Only mildly apologetic, the officer explained that, unfortunately, there had been a "breakdown in communications" that Saturday and the night shift had never gotten the message to show up. When the day shift's time was up, they'd driven off without waiting for their replacements, leaving Hillary to her own devices.

Outraged, Hillary slammed down the receiver and called an uncle at one of the city's older law firms and explained her predicament. The uncle told her to come in to his office. He'd fix everything.

Wearing a coat and tie for the occasion, Gil Lewis was taking in the view of the harbor from the uncle's elegant high-rise offices when Hillary arrived. The uncle, a stiff but kindly old gentleman, made the introductions, then discreetly excused himself when his niece began telling Lewis what the rapist had done to her that previous Friday night.

"Hillary was terrific," says Lewis, "really sophisticated and classy. A lot of rape victims clam up and can't talk about what happened, but Hillary told it just the way it occurred—exactly the way I would have. She was very direct. She was calm, but my God—with a rapist out there threatening to kill her sister and all her relatives, a guy whom she seduced over the phone into coming back, and the cops not doing a damn thing about it—that's pretty hard to take!

"If I'd been on the case earlier, I'd have told her, Look, don't go home unless the cops are *right there in the room with you*. I know how they can fuck up. Those guys are buried. They've probably got fifteen cases going on, and they're taking all kinds of shit from their sergeant, and it's a hot night, and they're probably all moonlighting anyway. So they say, Fuck it. I know them. When their time's up, they're *gone*."

Overworked as they are, Lewis knew they wouldn't appreciate a private investigator's coming in to help them out. "They don't want anyone else on the case for fear that their mistakes will be highlighted by someone else's success," he says. "I figured, If they resent my being there, why create heat?" So with Bingham, about all he'd do with the police was tell them where to make the arrest.

Lewis returned with Hillary to her apartment and had her walk through every step the rapist had made and to try to act out his gestures, the way he moved and walked. "That can tell you more about a guy than his hair or eye color," says Lewis. As she went through it all, the investigator noticed that, at least as Bingham reconstructed his actions, the rapist always kept his elbows close to his body and moved, in general, as though he were used to making his way around a tight space. "He seemed to be keeping from bumping into people," says Lewis.

The detective won't call it a "hunch," since he prefers to think that all his insights are based strictly on the evidence, but he felt certain that the rapist was, as he says, "a food guy"—someone who worked in a crowded kitchen.

He'd look into that, but for now he had to make sure that nothing further happened to Hillary. He figured she was all right at her office during the day, but he moved her out of her apartment and into the YWCA in the Back Bay to be safe at night. He'd keep watch over her the rest of the time himself—a "protective surveillance" he calls it. He also arranged with the phone company to put a tap on her phones to trace all incoming calls.

In the following weeks, he waited for her to emerge from her office building, looking in the reflective glass of the storefronts across the street. Then he followed her home on foot, always staying at least fifty feet back. When she went to a restaurant, he took a seat

several tables away. If she stopped to shop for clothes, he'd look over a rack on the other side of the store. He ended up concealing himself so well that for the first few days Hillary was sure he'd bailed out on her just like the police. Frantic, she called him up when she got home and was convinced he'd really stayed with her only when he reported what kind of salad she'd ordered for lunch.

When Hillary was safe at work, Lewis canvassed local restaurants, college dining halls, and hospital cafeterias to see if any of the personnel offices had hired anyone matching the rapist's striking description. "That scar on his forehead," Lewis notes, "was like a zipper. Anyone who'd seen him once would remember him forever."

Three weeks into the case, Lewis got a break. He found a hospital security chief who recognized the description. That scar! It belonged to a man named Federico Vargas who'd worked at the cafeteria grill, just as Lewis had suspected. Unfortunately, Vargas had quit a few weeks ago, so Lewis wouldn't find him at the hospital. But the chief produced a Dorchester address from his records.

Lewis drove by the house that afternoon. A shingled triple-decker, it still had Vargas' name on the mailbox.

One of Lewis' few confidants at the police department checked criminal records for him and said that a Federico Vargas was wanted in Texas for raping a fifteen-year-old.

Lewis knew that it would go far better in any trial if somehow this Vargas could be caught in the act—either of making a menacing call or of approaching Hillary Bingham. "I always keep the court in mind," he says. "I didn't just have to catch the guy. I had to put him away."

A few days after Lewis heard about Vargas, Bingham received a call on her office line and recognized, once again, her assailant. Following Lewis' instructions, she told the man she was busy in an office meeting and asked him to call her back in an hour. Then she dialed Lewis, who quickly checked with the phone company and found out that the call had come from a Dorchester pay phone at the corner of Eighth and Weld.

Now it was time to bring in the cops. He reached the lieutenant who had worked on the case initially, explained the latest developments, and asked him to send out some men to watch the Dorchester corner for a man fitting the rapist's description going into the phone booth.

Because of his private-citizen status, Lewis can arrest someone only in the act of committing a felony. He'd just as soon leave himself out of that part anyway. "The cops are paid to stop the bullets," he says, "not me."

An hour later, Bingham's phone rang again. Her caller berated her viciously for turning on him the way she had at her apartment. She forced out an apology to keep him on the line; then she heard shouts and sounds of a scuffle, and the line seemed to go dead. Then another voice came on. "Miss Bingham? This is Sergeant Walters of the Boston Police. We have just arrested your assailant."

———

Lewis doesn't gloat about besting the police detectives on the Bingham case, saying that the only satisfaction he takes from it comes from helping out a "good broad." He's not inclined to worry about the competition. In his business it doesn't pay to develop grudges, for he has to go where the money takes him. He's like the free-agent baseball player who knocks himself out for one team one season, then plays just as hard to beat them the next.

He has had to work against the police countless times on defense investigations, but ever since the career-launching Nugent affair he's often worked *for* them too, defending them from allegations of police brutality, corruption, and other crimes. "I go just as hard," he says, "either way."

Lewis has to steer clear of abiding loyalties. "That's a luxury I can't afford," he says. As long as he sticks to the terms of his license, Lewis can be free to roam. And he occasionally wanders into some gray areas.

He doesn't, for instance, mind working for clients who he senses have indeed committed the crimes they're charged with. Some of his police clients, for instance, were undoubtedly guilty—like the uniformed duo caught with their hands in the till at a Chinese restaurant early one morning, and the police ring accused of shaking down Back Bay homosexuals for protection money. Some were innocent. It's all the same to him. "I take each case as it comes," he says.

80

"I don't care who I do the work for," he goes on, "or who it takes me up against. I've helped out bad guys—child-molesters, Mafiosos, rapists, hit men—just as much as good ones. Someone once asked me, 'Doesn't it make you feel good to wear the white hat once in a while?' I said of course not. I don't see it that way. I don't care if they're guilty, or what they're guilty of. In my book, everyone's entitled to a defense. It's up to the courts to establish guilt or innocence. That's not my job. I'm not the judge, I'm the investigator.

"I'll tell you about a case," he adds, "that would have made anybody else squirm. A lot of people would have said I'd done the wrong thing, and maybe I did, but I did what I had to do."

A phone call brought Lewis into the company of an aged and rather tattered couple by the name of Mr. and Mrs. Harold Roth at the plush offices of a local attorney. The two sat together uneasily on the thick gray couch beside their lawyer's walnut desk, as large and shiny as a Cadillac. The sleeves on Mrs. Roth's raveled sweater dangled past her knuckles; the pin stripes on her husband's coat and trousers didn't match.

After the introductions, the Roths explained that they owned several apartment buildings in the seedier sections of town. In the last few years, they went on, three of them had gone up in smoke, and as if that weren't bad enough, a black man named James Silks had spun out a story in a lower court that the Roths had paid him to burn them. The judge had believed Silks' testimony and found the Roths guilty of arson. The couple had appealed the case to Superior Court, where they'd be tried by a jury. The week before, Silks had approached them to demand $500; if they didn't give him the money, he said, he was going to lay on his Superior Court testimony thicker than ever.

"Is there any truth to it?" asked Lewis finally. "Did you have those buildings torched?"

"No, no, no!" exclaimed Mr. Roth, stamping his foot on the wall-to-wall carpet. "We did nothing of the kind, I tell you—*nothing*. Vandals set those fires, I'm sure of it. A hundred times I have chased them out of my buildings. They hate us, Mr. Lewis, because we're white. They want to drive us out of the neighborhood, but we have no place else to go!"

Lewis has doubts about everyone, but he had particular doubts about the Roths. He knew there must have been something to Silks' story or the D.A. wouldn't have gone for it, let alone the judge. He also knew it was common practice for landlords to cut their losses in a declining neighborhood by setting their property on fire for the insurance money. But he knew that if he proved Silks guilty of blackmail, it would ruin Silks as a witness and wreck the government's action.

Lewis decided to take the case. He arranged for the cash transaction to take place in front of a diner where the Roths often had lunch. Lewis parked a short distance up the street, with photographer Duane Smith crouching in the back seat. Smith set up his camera at the rear window, shrouded with coats and perched in a bag of popcorn for stability. He got two dozen shots as Silks approached, spoke briefly with Mrs. Roth by the diner, and shook hands with her and the money flashed across. Silks stole a look at the $100 bills; then, just as Lewis had anticipated, he headed across the street to the bank to get change. After he came out, the detective went in, retrieved the bills, and compared them with a Xerox copy he'd made. They matched to the last digit.

Lewis passed the evidence on to the Roths' attorney, who saw that it came to the attention of the D.A. When it did, the government dropped all charges.

The Roths asked Lewis to meet them at the airport to collect his $250 fee on the case. When they approached him in the lobby, Lewis hardly recognized them. They now wore silk, mink, and diamonds and were headed to Miami Beach, they explained, to check out some of their other holdings and to celebrate. They thanked the detective profusely as they handed over his check. Then they scurried off to their boarding gate arm in arm.

Lewis was left with few doubts as to the Roths' dishonesty, but he expresses no remorse about letting the couple go free.

"I'm not Captain Marvel," he says. "I live in a world of practicality, not of romance. I'm there to do a specific job—to discover the facts. I can't worry about what happens after that. I'm not a crusader. Look, captains of industry may be guilty of price-fixing right now. People are starving to death somewhere. I can't worry about that. My job isn't to right all society's wrongs. I work under license. I'm obliged to tell the truth, and I do. I can't moralize. The government is far better equipped to make its case than I am. If they blow it, then shame on them. They should demand better police work. Maybe next time they won't pin their hopes on an extortionist and do the job right.

"I may have had a feeling in this case that those landlords were torching their buildings, but how was I to know for sure? Does that mean they aren't entitled to the best defense possible? Does that mean that I can only work for people I think are innocent? What kind of justice is that? Who knows—maybe there were extenuating circumstances: medical bills, death in the family—who knows? I just collect the facts. And the facts were that that guy took the extortion money. I have the photographs, and I have the bills to prove it. Those are the facts. The rest is just guesswork and philosophy. It isn't worth smoke!"

But there are facts and there are facts. Not all of them end up letting criminals off the hook. And even Lewis admits he's a lot happier with the ones that don't. He won't just poke around the city, he'll search the whole *country* for those.

"Everybody is missing somebody."

SEVEN

Hide and Seek

Number 1041 Ocean Drive in Laguna Beach, California, was a Spanish compound on a bluff by the sea; a miniature San Clemente, with red tile roofs, stucco walls, and arched doorways. Flowering plants bloomed everywhere. Lewis had to sidestep a trio of platinum-blond nymphets rolling by on skateboards to make it safely from his car to the slate path leading to the compound's front door.

The detective had flown out to check on his only lead in a Brockton, Massachusetts, missing-persons case. Lewis never knows

where the trail of the missing will lead; there is hardly a state in the country that he hasn't searched at one time or another trying to locate somebody. Back in Massachusetts, Margie Bryant, a likable thirty-nine-year-old waitress, had hired him to find her father, a man she hadn't seen since she was six, when her mother skipped out on him with little Margie in tow. Margie had always had warm memories of his taking her on fishing trips to nearby lakes and streams and telling her bedtime stories. But her mother had always answered her questions about him with a curt "What do you want to know about *him* for?" Her mother was dead now, though, and Margie wanted to find him. Still single, she didn't have anybody else.

From her birth certificate, Margie was able to tell Lewis her father's name, Wendell Atkins, as well as his address and occupation at the time of her birth. Now, almost forty years later, those bits of information led Lewis nowhere. The old home, he found out, had been leveled for a highway, and the foundry where Atkins used to work had burned. Wendell could have gone anywhere; he could be dead for all Lewis knew. It had been a long time.

But Margie recalled, vaguely, something about an aunt in California, and Lewis' call to the California registry miraculously produced a Shelly Atkins of approximately the right age on Ocean Drive. A phone call to the woman, asking for Wendell Atkins, elicited only a scratchy "Wendell *who?*" But there was something in the old lady's response that told Lewis she knew more than she was letting on. So, on a gamble, he'd flown out.

Chimes tinkled when Lewis pressed the bell, and a graying woman in a loose-fitting dress answered the door.

"Yes?"

"Sorry to bother you, ma'am," said Lewis politely, peeling off his sunglasses, "but could you tell me which way it is to the center of town? I'm totally lost."

As he spoke, he stole a look behind the old woman to check out the interior decor—expensive—and to check for other occupants—none. This must be Shelly Atkins. As if to confirm it, the lady replied as brusquely as the woman on the phone. "That way," she said, pointing down the street. Then she closed the door.

Lewis didn't mind the snub, since he had other ways to get the information he needed. He drove to the Laguna Beach Civic Center and made straight for the sanitation department. He explained to the sunburned clerk that he had just moved into Ocean Drive and would like to know the times of the city trash collections. "Tuesday and Friday mornings," replied the clerk after consulting a manila folder.

Good timing. This was Monday. Back at his motel, he set his alarm for 3 A.M. Miss Atkins would have her trash collected a little early this week.

When Lewis had filched the trash of a Philadelphia Appeals Court judge, he had dressed in sneakers and a tattered raincoat. But nobody dresses like that in Laguna Beach, so when the alarm sounded, he just put on a T-shirt and blue jeans and drove his rented Mazda out to Ocean Drive. He feigned interest in the neighboring rubbish barrels for a moment or two, then descended on the overstuffed plastic bins of Shelly Atkins. He deftly popped her two heavy-duty Glad bags into the trunk and returned to the motel, where he dumped them out onto four sheets of newspaper spread out over the wall-to-wall carpeting. He pulled on surgical gloves to keep his hands clean and separated the rubbish into three piles: genuine garbage like chicken bones and artichoke leaves; potentially useful material, such as junk mail and magazine wrappers; and items of "true value." That third category held precisely one item, and Lewis held it up to the light like a gold nugget. It was an envelope bearing a return address in the upper left-hand corner. *Wendell Atkins,* it said, *RFD 517, Yakima, Washington.*

Lewis wrapped up the rest of the junk in the newspapers, stuffed it into a trash barrel, and waited eagerly for sunrise, when he could wire his bank for money for a trip to Yakima to check out Wendell Atkins in person. "I always want to be sure," he says.

Money in hand the next day, he flew to Seattle and rented a Pinto for the long drive through the mountains to Yakima. He found out Atkins' street address by inquiring at the post office about his "old friend" and, with the help of a couple of gas-station attendants, found the place up in the hills on the outskirts of town. Built of stout oak and rock, the house looked as if it had been there forever. There was even a good-sized orchard out back.

A tall, reedy man with glacier-white hair answered Lewis' knock on the door. He pretended, once again, that he was lost. When the gentleman started to give directions back to town, Lewis interrupted him.

"Say," he asked, "do I detect a New England accent?"

"You certainly do," replied the man proudly. "I was born and raised in Massachusetts, but that's a long time ago now. Why—you from the East?"

Lewis replied that he was from Boston and he was out here on business. Pleased to find a countryman, the man invited Lewis inside. Once in the living room, the detective didn't take a seat, even after his host handed him a glass of apple juice. "You get a lot more if you keep standing," explains the detective. "Then they don't have to worry you're never going to leave." While it might have been easier simply to ask the man his name point-blank, Lewis preferred less direct means. "I didn't want to spook him," he says.

Instead, seeing a fly rod in the corner, Lewis asked about the fishing in these parts. Margie had said something about her father's devotion to the sport. That got him talking, and the two chatted amiably for half an hour. By that time, the gentleman had dropped so many details about his old house in Massachusetts and his years at the foundry that Lewis knew this had to be Wendell Atkins.

Three weeks later another unexpected visitor appeared at Atkins' door. "Dad?" she said. "It's me, Margie."

It took a moment for the old man's mind to run back to the daughter he hadn't seen for so long.

"Margie!" Atkins shouted, and wrapped his arms around her. The two clung to each other for a long time without speaking. "I can't believe it's you," Atkins said finally. "I just can't believe it."

Lewis received a letter from the old fly fisherman a while later complimenting him on "a truly remarkable action of master detective work worthy of Sherlock Holmes." Lewis filed it with the rest of his notes on the case. He was grateful for the compliment, but never responded. "Atkins never guessed I was the stranger who came to his house for directions," says Lewis. "I figured—why complicate it?"

——

"Everybody is missing somebody," says Lewis. It's an old friend, maybe; a distant cousin; a childhood sweetheart. Gradually, like astronauts journeying to the far side of the moon, people just drift out of contact. Letters come back ADDRESSEE UNKNOWN; telephone calls get the familiar recording, "We're sorry. The number you have dialed has been disconnected."

A kind of death, perhaps, but it's a natural passing of friends nowadays, and few can afford to hire Lewis to try to reestablish the connection. He enters into this twilight zone only when the disappearances are more sudden, or more painful. He has worked for the children of broken homes, like Margie Bryant, trying, years later, to put the fragments back together and for adopted kids searching for their natural parents. A few clients have been lonelyhearts who have perhaps fallen for a stranger in a singles bar. And increasingly, older people have come to him. Alone, with time on their hands, they are longing to see a child who's moved, or an ex-husband, or sometimes even a childhood friend. More mysterious are the cases of husbands, or wives, who have awakened one morning to find the bed empty beside them.

The sort of missing person who interests Lewis the most (partly because the detective himself would never do such a thing) is the one who decides he just can't take it anymore and rides on out. This type of escapee changes with the times. In the youth rebellion of the late sixties, it was mostly teen-agers who cut out this way. "Back then," says Lewis, "I felt like I was spending all my time showing snapshots of kids to my old friends at Greyhound Bus." With the feminist movement, the majority of escapees these days are middle-aged, married women eager to strike out on their own. For some of these women, sudden disappearance is the only way out.

One confided to Lewis that when she'd told her husband she wanted a divorce, he'd pulled out his revolver and pointed it at her head. "Divorce?" he said. "Meet my lawyers, Smith and Wesson." Then he pulled the trigger. Mercifully, the gun wasn't loaded, but that was when the lady figured it was time to go. By this time, actually, Lewis' reputation in missing persons was so well established he was not hired by the husband to track his departed wife, but by the wife herself—she wanted instructions on how to disappear. He told her: while she could keep her name, she should change a digit of her Social Security number—that way her husband couldn't track her through the federal computer (she would be able to collect her Social Security payments when she needed them later by showing her work records and claiming to have made an honest mistake); rent an apartment in a friend's name so she couldn't be traced through her own; register any new set of license plates to her husband's address, since registration information is hardly leak-proof, as Lewis well knew; and not to install a telephone, for the number, even if unlisted, would get back to her husband somehow. Although she stayed within the state, she sank without a trace. Her husband still hasn't a clue to where she is.

"People leave because they feel pressure," says Lewis. As with the Smith & Wesson business, it's not always hard to see where the pressure is coming from. Lewis found the owner of a New Jersey greeting-card company in New York City working under an assumed name as a short-order cook. He had been facing bankruptcy proceedings. Lewis learned the secret of a vanished accountant in a few minutes' conversation with the abandoned wife. "She griped about how he never picked up his clothes, never paid her any attention, and had only married her for her money," Lewis recalls. "Then she told me she'd fix that asshole by getting him arrested for nonsupport. I'm surprised he didn't leave sooner." Worst of all though, was the man who skipped out on his wife when she came down with terminal cancer. But some cases remain inexplicable. "How," asks Lewis with a laugh, "do you figure the guy who leaves his wife because she's too religious only to run off to Sarasota with a nun?"

Of the nearly two hundred such persons Lewis has hunted for in his career, he had turned up all but five, and he has reason to believe that all of those five are dead. So confident is he of his talents that he offers his clients a guarantee: All they pay up front is a few hundred to cover expenses. He won't charge for his time until he "makes the location." At that point, his customers are only too happy to kick in the few-thousand-dollar finder's fee in exchange for the precious address. "When I make the find," says Lewis, "I tell the client, 'Send me a check and I'll tell you where the guy is. If it's not him, stop the check.'" Lewis has always collected.

With such a track record, Lewis doesn't have to worry about the competition. The police are certainly no threat. "Unless there's evidence of a kidnapping, their hands are tied because of their jurisdiction," says Lewis. "Once the guy leaves town, forget it." Adopted children and abandoned wives can turn to a few specialized agencies for help, but hardly any institution serves the full range of Lewis' clients.

In desperation, many searchers turn to psychics. "They take your money," says Lewis, "and then tell you they see 'water' or 'a rectangular shape.' Not too helpful. I'd been investigating the disappearance of a seven-year-old kid for three months one time when I heard that a psychic had come onto some talk show and had a vision about the case. She said she could see the kid near water with a head wound. So the talk-show host called up the state police and *insisted* they fly her over the town in a helicopter so she could get a reading, like a human divining rod. The cops sent her up, and ran out a pack of bloodhounds, but they never turned up a thing. The body showed up later in a footlocker in Danvers. Why is everyone so eager to believe in magic? Those people aren't psychics, they're *psychos*."

For Lewis, there is nothing occult involved in tracking missing persons. He figures if he can establish two of what he terms the "basic four" items—full name, age, previous address, and place of education—right off, he's home free. Unable to make a complete break with the past, the majority of the missing retain their names, so that's a good start right there. Many of the rest just shift to a middle name. Married women often return to their maiden names.

With a name to go on, Lewis can start tracking what he calls "life signs"—the bills, records, receipts, and job or credit applications that all the living leave behind. And even the lightest traveler takes along a highly traceable collection of habits, memberships, friends, associations, and hobbies. Those who deliberately go into hiding are no exception. They inevitably slip up by making collect phone calls to old friends, or "safe" relatives—their town and phone number showing up on the relatives' toll receipts. Like Wendell Atkins, they may write letters with a return address or, at least, a postmark on the canceled stamp. They use old credit cards or write a check on their old bank account, or buy a car, entering their names with a state registry. They give the name of an old employer as an employment or credit reference. They join a new branch of their old club—Rotarians, Elks—or old church denomination. They keep in touch with an alumni association. Or, possibly, they are remarkably cautious and do none of this—but run off with a friend or lover who isn't so careful.

No one ever makes a clean break, and it's touching to see which ties end up binding. Lewis has found several long-term absentees by staking out their mother's grave on Thanksgiving or her birthday.

There are many ways to follow the bread crumbs these wanderers leave behind. Lewis developed his trash technique in a two-year undercover investigation for a media conglomerate whose license to run its TV station had been revoked by the FCC and awarded to a competitor. Appealing the decision, the conglomerate hired Lewis, along with its best investigative reporters, to dig up some dirt on the opposition. Lewis scooped them all by dispatching Grove to nip the competitor's refuse from its dumpster before the trash collector came. There Lewis read volumes in confidential memos, first drafts, letters, notes, telephone-call slips, even the carbon typewriter ribbons. All of it, Lewis stresses, "legally abandoned property."

"You can't overestimate the value of trash," he goes on. It's clinched any number of his missing-persons cases, like Wendell Atkins', just as it's helped with background checks, by providing a way to extract information from people who aren't disposed toward giving it.

Lewis' only data bank for missing-persons work is a branch of the Boston Public Library which has copies of many of the high school and college yearbooks published in the United States. They are particularly useful for photographs, possible occupations, classmates' names and home addresses. The library also has a stock of old city directories and telephone books from around the country. But for the most part, Lewis can track the missing in the privacy of his own home, where he curls up in the big brown chair in the corner of his living room with his telephones—the red one that's connected to the answering service, the regular black one with his private line. When he was just starting out in the business,

91

it took him a hundred calls to get anywhere on a case. Now, armed with the right information, he can zero in on his man in twenty.

He has several times done it in one—by calling Directory Assistance in the city of the departed's last known address. "You'd be surprised how many people never think to try that," he says.

But he has done more complicated locations almost as quickly. One was for an elderly man calling from Schenectady to say he hadn't heard from his brother Clement in fifty-five years. Pressed for more information, the man explained that his name was Albert Henderson and his parents had been killed in a car crash in Bainbridge, Ohio, when he was eight. He'd been packed off to live with an uncle in Schenectady, and never found out what happened to his brother. "I'm getting on in years, Mr. Lewis," said the caller. "It would mean so much to me if I could see Clement again."

Exactly one hour later, Lewis called Henderson back to tell him he could reach his brother in Oak Ridge, Tennessee, where he was serving as a district court judge, and he gave him the number.

There was a long silence on the other end of the line. "I don't know how I can ever thank you," Henderson said finally.

Lewis didn't want him even to try. "The case was too easy," he says. All he'd done was call the chief of the Bainbridge Police, generally a good source of information in any small town. Chief Mazur in fact turned out to have been a pallbearer at the senior Hendersons' funeral. He remembered that Clement had gone off to live with an aunt at Oak Ridge, although he hadn't heard from him since. Lewis then called the Oak Ridge police department to consult their citizens' directory, but the officer who answered the night phone didn't need to refer to it. "Everybody knows Judge Henderson," he said.

Telephone sources aren't always so forthcoming, though. Registries of motor vehicles around the country, for instance, are peerless resources, but aren't inclined to dispense registrants' names and addresses to all and sundry. "Otherwise," says Lewis, "every time a guy saw a good-looking broad on the highway . . ." Some states insist that requests be made in writing; others will give the information on the phone, but the caller has to give the right password first. The Massachusetts code word one year was "inflation." The code word is used by local police in the state when requesting information. "So I'd call up the registry," Lewis explains, "say 'inflation,' and then tell them this was Andover calling for a check on, say, Mass plate QE-743. I'd wait a few minutes, and they'd give the information right back to me. To find out the new code, I call up the Andover police and say I'm from the registry, do they have the new code yet? Oh, you do; well, would you read it back to me? They give me a read-back every time."

On calls in which he has to identify himself, he gives a variety of all-American names, none of them his own. "Usually I say I'm Bob Wilson," Lewis explains, "since there are probably hundreds of Bob Wilsons around, and it's so easy to get confused with other names. They'll be asking themselves for hours afterward, 'Was that Will Bobson? Rob Nielson? John Williamson?' I try to say it fast. To get hospital records, I'll be Dr. Wilson, because hospital workers always respond to doctors, or I might say I'm Bob Wilson from Accounting. For bank records, I'm Bob Wilson, a loan officer from another branch of the bank. To get personal information calling someone's house, I say I'm Bob Wilson of Universal Energy Consultants and that I'm looking into local conservation efforts. I ask 'em a few things about their heating systems and insulation, then get into the stuff I really want to know. If I want to get an address out of somebody's family I say I'm Bob Wilson from the Alumni Committee and that I'm arranging a college reunion. If it's a state agency, I say I'm Bob Wilson calling from the Governor's office. That really makes them quake.

"No, it doesn't bother me to pull the wool over people's eyes. I love it. I'm sitting there in my underwear in my living room with a two-day beard, and they're thinking I'm this big bureaucrat who's going to owe them a favor. It turns the tables on the whole ass-kissing system."

But Lewis will never pass himself off as a cop. From time to time, he will freely give the *impression* that he's with the police—in person by the imposing way he stands, on the phone by indicating he's "from Andover"—but he'll never come out and say it. "There's a good reason for that," he snaps. "It's illegal."

The key to a successful con job, Lewis explains, is sounding impatient. "You make it clear to the guy that it's got to be done *right away*." That means Lewis has to be quick with the questions on his end. He keeps a list of Wollaston pay-phone numbers handy in case somebody insists on calling him back, to verify, say, that this really *is* Bob Wilson from the American Geological Society. "That doesn't happen too often," says Lewis, "but when it does, I tell the guy to give me a few minutes because I've got to make another call; then I dash downtown to hit the phone box before they ring."

"Roger really knows how to do it," Lewis goes on. "He's kind of meek in person, but on the phone it's a different story." Grove generally insists on privacy for his calls, but Lewis once caught him in action and was surprised to see his younger associate gesturing wildly with his free hand as he spoke firmly into the receiver. The voice was fierce and imperious, almost tyrannical. "It was like a whole new Roger," marvels the detective.

When he wants to, Lewis genuinely sounds like a bureaucrat, but his voice has just enough sweetness in it to encourage people to tell all they know. Indeed, once some of them get started, there's almost no stopping them. They start reading out privileged information from the computer, and it can get pretty interesting. "I might ask a lab technician about a patient's leg fracture in 1969," Lewis says, "but he'll start telling me about the appendectomy in '58, the measles in '56, the whooping cough in '52, the mother's emphysema, the sister's miscarriage, the parents' divorce. I'm the one who has to say I've gotta run, or they'd go on forever."

As a convenience, Lewis has cultivated a number of friends at various agencies around town—the phone company for those indispensable toll slips, credit-card companies for the charge receipts, some of the major banks for withdrawal information, and the police department for a rundown on someone's criminal record. "I take them out to dinner every year around Christmas," Lewis explains. "Afterwards I give them a present to remember me by—maybe a bottle of Chivas Regal or a radio." They never forget a friend.

When Lewis has to confront a source in person, he always makes

94

it clear that it's not *his* idea to ask these questions, it's the boss back at the office. "I tell them, 'Look, I've just *got* to ask you . . .' " Generally, simple self-confidence is enough to carry off any impersonation. Once, in the Caribbean, he got a look at the plans for a new house—and a good estimate of the owner's income Lewis needed for a divorce case—by strolling up to the construction site and explaining he was an architect himself back home and would anybody mind if he took a look around?

In the TV license fight, he got reams of credit information about one of the principals by passing himself off as the man himself, with only an envelope filched from the subject's trash to back him up. Another time, he took a calling card from the desk of a bank president to use as a kind of passkey to the record room downstairs. And he improvises. To get a look at a record book in an office building, he pulled Grove over to him in the lobby for a deep discussion just as the cleaning lady was going by with her mops one night. "I told the lady," Lewis recalls, " 'I'm really wrapped up right now with my aide—would you mind bringing me that record book I left on my desk in 26E?' "

Only once in a missing-persons case has he ever left his true identity any great distance behind him. In the early seventies Lewis was hired by a well-to-do Concord couple to find their teenage daughter, Diane Randolph, after she was a week late returning home from her Swiss boarding school. Lewis usually advises parents to wait for runaways to come back by themselves, which most do within six months. "If I have to drag the kids back," Lewis says, "they aren't likely to stay put for long." And Lewis tires quickly of repeat performances. Worse, since they rarely use credit cards, install their own telephones, or buy cars, kids are hard to track. But the Randolphs made it worth his while.

An old friend from Diane's elementary school produced Lewis' only lead in the case when she confided that Diane used to hang out with a sometime Harvard student and drifter named Jay Jencks in Harvard Square.

"Trouble was," Lewis says, "Harvard University is even tighter than the CIA when it comes to doling out information about one of their own." But a Cambridge cop gave Lewis the tip that Jencks was known to spend his days spare-changing in the middle of Harvard Square with some of his frizzed-out friends. He gave Lewis a description. When a two-day stakeout didn't produce Jencks, Lewis had to try something bolder.

Since the hippies weren't likely to warm to a graying detective asking questions about a comrade, Lewis figured he'd have to infiltrate. He purchased a black-and-white-striped bed sheet at a department-store white sale, cut a hole out of it for his head, dirtied it up, and threw it on over his shoulders like a poncho.

That evening, in his sheet, he ditched his Buick on a side street and ambled up to a gray frame house near Harvard Square. He had turned up runaways in such places before; found one of them *in flagrante* with a fellow traveler in an upstairs bathtub. This time, the house was vacant except for the cockroaches, so Lewis sat on the barren floor and waited. At ten, a gang of communards drifted in on a cloud of marijuana smoke wearing an assortment of Eastern garb. They greeted Lewis in his bed sheet cheerfully—"Hey, man, how ya doin'?"

Lewis merely extended a kind of papal wave without speaking. "Oh, wow," responded one hipster. "Hey, that's *cool.*" Thinking they were out of earshot, others wondered out loud, "What's *his* trip?" One of them got a little sassy: Patty, Lewis later discovered, a strawberry blonde from the Bronx. "Hey, holy man, what you got under that sheet?" she asked, reaching out to peek at his divine underclothes. The detective grabbed her firmly by the wrist and, in a vaguely Roman gesture, extended his hand outward from his chest. Awestruck, Patty nicknamed Lewis "Shana Ru" and fed him a dinner of bean sprouts and carrot cake. Lewis, however, remained impartial, smiling his Maharishi smile to all comers.

Lewis became a regular fixture on the living-room floor the next few days. The group offered him tokes on their water pipes and takeout bags full of cheeseburgers and vanilla frappes, but gave out no information about Jay Jencks or Diane Randolph. So Lewis decided to force the issue by leaving a snapshot of Diane on the floor one evening before the gang trooped home. Some time went by before anyone noticed it. Then a kid in a flak jacket yelped, "Hey! Where'd *this* come from?" and the whole gang gathered around. "I know that chick," added a friend; "I just saw her yesterday." But that was all she volunteered.

96

Fortunately, before Lewis had to break his vow of silence—and his cover—to ask where, Patty popped the question for him.

"On the Common," replied the flower child. "You know, on the benches by the monument. Man, was she wired. That cat Jay was with her."

Clad in his sheet, with only a sweater and a pair of Bermuda shorts underneath to keep out the midwinter cold, Lewis staked out the monument the next afternoon. Diane didn't show up, unfortunately, but her boyfriend Jay did. The few hairs left on his balding head were wound tightly together in a ponytail. The detective tailed him to a nearby bar and waited through Happy Hour till Jencks came back out, climbed quickly into a parked car, and drove off. But the all-seeing Shana Ru got the license number.

The car belonged to a Boston University professor. On a gamble, Lewis called the man the next day to say he was Dr. Wilson from the University of Massachusetts and that a Jay Jencks had just applied for a job using the professor as a reference. He didn't happen to have Jencks's current address, did he? The professor did indeed—on Grover Street.

Two days of automobile surveillance produced regular sightings of the ponytailed Jencks and—at last—of the starry-eyed Diane Randolph. Lewis phoned in the address to the girl's parents, who swooped down from Concord immediately to retrieve their wayward daughter. Lewis retired his bed sheet.

———

Of all the things he does, Lewis likes his missing-persons work best. While he is proud to be able to do so much with such meager resources, these cases call up in him something deeper than pride. Pulling other people's families back together, he must recall his own childhood, when he felt so estranged from his parents, brothers, and sisters. He became a loner then, he stayed a loner throughout his marriage, and he's a loner still. With the missing-persons work, he can undo such twists of fate for others. And so these searches for the departed aren't so much treks across the landscape as they are trips back through time, back to the point in the life of the family where the first breach occurred.

That was what he was hoping to do for the shy, quiet teen-ager with long brown hair named Felicia Solito. "A funny, gentle kid," he says, "a whole lot different from that bratty Diane Randolph. I really wanted the best for her." She came to him to find her father, who'd run out on the family even before Felicia was born. Her mother, who gave Felicia her own last name after her husband took off for Reno, had died a few years afterward, leaving her daughter to be brought up by a grandfather in Quincy. When he died, Felicia was taken in by an aunt who already had three growing children of her own. Now seventeen, she had been jilted by her first serious boyfriend, and she felt she had no one. She'd saved up a little more than $30 for the detective, but Lewis merely smiled and told her to put her money away.

"Just tell me everything you know about your father," he said.

That, it turned out, was very little: only a first name, Jim; the vague idea he'd worked for a Quincy shipbuilder; and the rumor that he'd remarried a local girl and moved away. Probing her childhood memories, however, Lewis was able to add another fact when Felicia recalled that a family doctor had once startled her by calling her "Miss Edwards."

"That's your father's name right there," he said, "James Edwards."

But Lewis still had no idea where to find him. The Quincy shipyard was probably General Dynamics. But since the company handled defense contracts, information about old employees was classified. The town's Bureau of Vital Statistics had no record of her parents' 1961 marriage, and Felicia's birth certificate, obtained at the State House, listed only her mother's name.

Hoping that Edwards was still in the state, Lewis ran the name through the Registry of Motor Vehicles computer. It spewed out dozens of James Edwardses, three of them a likely age, but none panned out. So Lewis turned to the old city directories in the public library. He began with the 1962 volume, since that would list Edwards' address if he'd moved back to town after the divorce, and found a James Edwards at 13 Maple Street. Working with the rumor about a second wife, Lewis now hurried back to the Bureau of Vital Statistics to try to match this Maple Street Edwards with a marriage license after '62. Sure enough, in 1964, James Edwards, an engineer residing at 13 Maple, had married Margery O'Connor. Better yet, the license also recorded the bridegroom's parents—Mr. and Mrs. Eugene Edwards of Enosburg Falls, Vermont.

Lewis dialed Vermont information and determined that the Edwardses were still in residence. When he reached Mrs. Eugene Edwards, he introduced himself as Bob Wilson from the American Engineering Society. The Society had lost track of her son, he explained. Did Mrs. Edwards have a current address? The old woman had to put down the receiver to find her address book before uttering the magic words: 53 Shoreline Drive, Charleston, South Carolina 29401. She also had a phone number and business address.

To make sure this James Edwards was really Felicia's father, Lewis dialed Charleston. Speaking with a slight drawl, Edwards himself answered. This time Lewis said he was organizing a reunion of the General Dynamics workers of 1961 for the spring.

Edwards answered right off that he wasn't interested.

"But you did work at General Dynamics?" pursued the detective.

"Hell yes," answered Edwards. "Worst job I ever had."

It appeared that this was the right James Edwards.

When Felicia heard that Lewis had found her father, she made plans to fly to Charleston with a girlfriend. Lewis picked up the tab.

While the friend waited at the corner, Felicia walked up Shoreline Drive to Number 53. She wasn't planning to jump into her father's arms or anything, she told Lewis. She didn't even intend to let on who she was. She just wanted to see him.

The house was enormous, with a fancy gabled roof and a broad green lawn. When Felicia rang the doorbell, a little girl with a ponytail and a Southern accent answered. The pauper and the princess eye to eye. Felicia hadn't planned on this—somehow she'd expected her father to come to the door. She didn't have the nerve to ask for him, but following Lewis' instructions, she mumbled that she was lost and needed directions back to the highway. The girl said she was alone in the house and wasn't supposed to speak to strangers. She was sorry but she had to close the door. Felicia flew back home in tears.

Taking matters into his own hands, Lewis had his attorney send

Edwards a registered letter asking him to a meeting with his daughter, Felicia Solito.

"Does she want money?" asked Edwards in an agitated phone call.

"No, just to meet you," the attorney assured him. Finally, Edwards agreed that if Felicia signed away all rights to support, he'd meet with her. Once.

Felicia sent the letter the next day. "I wasn't surprised he pulled something like that," she said. "After all, he'd run out on my mother. But I still wanted to meet him."

Edwards flew to Boston two weeks later. He met Felicia at the airport, then took her to lunch at a restaurant by the water. Lewis followed the two in his Buick and parked by the door so he could, as he says, "get a look at the son-of-a-bitch" when he walked by. The man was trim, Lewis saw, and handsome in a slicked-back sort of way, with a tight smile.

Not so surprisingly, the lunch was a disaster. Felicia was nervous and her father was ashamed. He'd suspected Felicia existed—her mother had been pregnant when he flew to Nevada for the divorce—but he hadn't known her name, or what she looked like. He was shocked to hear that his ex-wife was dead. He went on about his three daughters and the energy company he'd started down South, but Felicia could hardly bear to listen. He had a whole other life! Although she never let on, she was secretly hoping he'd change his mind and take her home with him to the luxury she'd seen down in Charleston. But it didn't happen.

Afraid she would burst into tears, she declined his offer of a ride home and stood outside the restaurant as he climbed into a taxi for the airport. She watched the taxi until it was out of sight, and then got into the car with Lewis.

Felicia wanted him to drive her to see her mother's grave on the way back. The detective stood back a little as Felicia went up to the low stone marker with her mother's name and knelt down beside it. "Momma," he heard Felicia say quietly, "I know who I am."

But after all that, she was still fatherless and alone. So Lewis figured the case would have to continue a little longer. He helped her out at first by giving her his extra typing work, then treated her to

100

guitar lessons, and finally, enrolled her in a community college. "I figured—why not? My own children were grown," he says. "With the agency going well, I had the extra money, and she's a good kid." Now, four years later, the two are frequently seen sitting together over breakfast at the Mug 'n' Muffin. They could be father and daughter—and extremely happy ones at that.

Another case closed.

"All you have in this business is your memories."

EIGHT

Gil and Howard

"The bigger a guy is," says Lewis, "the easier he is to find." He didn't think it would be any problem to locate Howard Hughes. Far from being cowed by the man's fabulous wealth, his eccentricity, his starlets, and the fact that no outsider had seen him in twenty years, Lewis would turn it all to his advantage.

"A lot of people might wonder, 'How do you find out if the richest guy in the world is still alive?' and they stop there," says the detective. "They just can't figure any way to attack it. But a celebrity can't hide. Everybody knows him. Hughes had books written about him, magazine stories, encyclopedia articles, newspaper gossip columns, and a million things. God, his footprints are probably engraved at Grauman's Chinese."

The *National Enquirer* put him onto the case back in March of 1976, just after Lewis had wrapped up the Elaine Noble affair. Bothered by competition from *Star* and *Midnight Sun*, the tabloid was eager for something to boost circulation and hoped that exclusive photographs of a billionaire hermit would do the trick. H.H., after all, was a *National Enquirer* natural: Hughes of Hughes Aircraft and TWA, of Las Vegas and California real estate, of RKO, the Spruce Goose, and Jane Russell's cantilevered bra. Now, after the Clifford Irving scandal, rumors abounded that despite those endless Kleenexes he used to protect his flesh from germs, the man was dead, or a vegetable, his hair down to his shoulders, his fingernails so long they were curling.

The *Enquirer*'s Boston stringer gave an impressive account of Lewis' missing-persons credentials, but the editors were troubled by the recent experience of a Canadian publisher who had paid an ex–CIA agent $50,000 to dig up proof that Hughes was dead or alive. The operative had taken the money, yet all he'd sent back was a postcard from South America saying he *thought* Hughes was alive but he couldn't be sure.

"The first I heard of it," Lewis recalls, "was when the *Enquirer* called me up to say they had some intriguing investigative work for me and could I give them some references. So I gave them the name of the state Attorney General, my friend Frank Bellotti. They called up Frank and then they called me back to ask me to run down a tip that young Joe Kennedy was shacked up with a broad somewhere in the Northeast.

"Nobody knew where Joe was living," Lewis goes on, "but I saw in the paper that there was going to be a big party at the Parker House, and the kid was supposed to attend. So I hung by the door watching for him, and followed him back afterwards. A broad was with him, and the two of them drove out to this brown three-decker in Cambridge. There was another car in the driveway. I ran the plates later and got the girl's name. But I had to stake the place out, to make sure she was the right one.

"There was no action that night, but the next day I found out what an impossible driver Kennedy was to follow. He must have been trained by the Secret Service in avoidance tactics, because once he hit the main drags, he'd open it up, then slow it down and change lanes and do forty miles an hour in the passing lane, so everyone would have to pass him on his right. I stuck with him, by staying in his blind spot, and I hung on him for about four or five days, but she was the only girl I ever saw. So I phoned the name in to the *Enquirer,* and they sent out a team of photographers in a van to get some pictures from across the street. But the funny part was, they never got a thing because the cops grabbed them all for loitering. They're pretty protective of the Kennedys around here."

Impressed with Lewis' work nonetheless, the editors put him through one more hoop, asking him to locate a Warren Commission witness who, thirteen years later, was living somewhere in West Germany. "I looked up some old magazine articles," says Lewis, "and got the names of some of the guy's relatives. I made a few calls and got the paper the address and phone number in about a week."

Finally, the editors told Lewis what they really wanted him to do, and even the cool and collected detective warmed up a few degrees. "It was my big chance," he says. He was sure he could make good on it. Confident of his investigative skills anyway, he also recalled some inside information that would make the job go a little easier.

Ten years before, Howard Hughes had rented a suite at Boston's Ritz-Carlton for six months while, depending on which report one believed, either he was receiving kidney treatments at Mass. General or he was consulting Boston brokers about how to invest the $546.5 million he'd just received in exchange for his TWA stock. Roger Grove was part of the security detail assigned to Hughes at the hotel. Good detectives never let such opportunities pass unexploited, and Grove had made the most of this one by copying down the license-plate numbers of all the cars in Hughes's considerable entourage, then tracing ownership through the registry. Although he never caught a glimpse of the retiring billionaire, he did memorize the faces of Hughes's close associates, the inner circle of devout Mormons dubbed "The Tabernacle." As Lewis says, "All you have in this business is your memories."

On March 29, the *Enquirer* flew Lewis down to its Lantana, Florida, headquarters to close the deal. Located near the sea, the office building was flamingo pink and surrounded by reflecting ponds. "A gossip factory covering half a football field," Lewis calls it. "All around me, I kept thinking, writers were banging out stories of three-headed chickens and commuting by UFO."

Lewis wasn't charmed by his editor, Gary Field, either. "A nickel-and-dime guy," he recalls. "Plus his hair was dyed solid auburn, all one color, like a rug." Still, Lewis was pleased with the terms he came away with: $50,000 for photographs of Hughes, unlimited expenses, and a 60–40 split in Lewis' favor on worldwide syndication of the photographs and an account of the story behind them. Another *Enquirer* editor told him later that the deal could

mean a quarter-million at least. However, the arrangement would have to be reviewed by *Enquirer* executives before it was final.

Back in Wollaston on March 31, Lewis got right to work tracking the billionaire whose whereabouts had stumped the world for two decades. Bright and early that morning he drove to the public library to look through the periodical index. Lewis found dozens of articles about Hughes, but he had to scan only a handful of them to find out everything he needed to know: names of Hughes's relatives, favorite retreats, and personal habits.

Armed with this information, Lewis returned home to stalk Hughes by phone. "The whole world did business with him," he says, "so I could pass myself off as just about anybody, even Wells Fargo. I called the places mentioned in the magazine articles, asking first for Howard, although I knew I didn't have much chance of getting through, and then for members of the Tabernacle. I knew all their names from Roger. The aides are never as secretive as the boss. I figured I'd find Howard by finding them."

Lewis always first-named the billionaire in his reminiscences. He always first-names everyone, of course, but with Hughes something more was involved. As the search went on, the detective began to feel an unexpected kinship with his prey. After his failed marriage and abandoned friendships, Hughes wasn't all that different from the detective himself—except for the size of their bank accounts. "But everybody just took Howard for a dollar sign," says Lewis. What with his own unusual career and reclusive life-style, Lewis sometimes felt he had a similar problem. In unguarded moments, Lewis even saw Hughes as a sort of rich uncle, particularly since Hughes's fortune would make Lewis'. Gil thought of it almost as an inheritance.

"I tried Howard's favorite hotel in Paradise Island off Florida," Lewis continues. "I tried his relatives in Texas. I tried various places in California. I tried Vegas. I was running up quite a phone bill, but I got nothing all around. No Howard. So then I called information in Salt Lake City. Since the inner circle were all Mormons, I figured that's where they'd live. And I was right, because I got home numbers for all five. And on the first call I got lucky."

When a female voice answered, Lewis asked for Bob.

"He's out of town, I'm afraid."

"Where is he—down on the islands?"

"No, he's in Acapulco."

"Oh, really," answered Lewis in a voice as smooth as Hughes's silk pajamas. "Where's he staying?"

"The usual—at the Princess."

"Is Howard with him?"

"Now, how would I know that?" drawled the wife.

"How about Bill?"

"Oh, yeah, he's there."

"Tom?"

"Yep."

"Pete?"

"Yeah. Now, say, just who is this, anyway?"

"Oh, I'm just one of Bob's business acquaintances. I'll try to catch him later. Thanks. Bye."

Gil Lewis had his billionaire—in the Princess Hotel in Acapulco, Mexico. And it was only three o'clock. The search had taken him all of six hours. Lewis pulled out a victory Coronella, lit up, leaned back, and breathed in the smoke with total satisfaction as though, for once, he were inhaling a real Havana.

"I try never to get ahead of myself," Lewis says now, "but that's when I started thinking about what would happen when I cashed in with Howard." He wasn't, he decided, looking forward to fame, exactly. Hughes's hermit existence frightened him off that, not to mention all the other celebrities (local ones, to be sure) whose lives came under Lewis' professional scrutiny. No, what he wanted out of the case was "the recognition." After laboring so diligently for so long in the shadows, Lewis simply wanted people to notice. So effectively had he cultivated his anonymity, he was beginning to feel imprisoned by it. Now, by snagging the world's most famous billionaire, he'd found a way to break out. "I was going to succeed where everybody else had failed," he says. "That was the best part. I'd finally prove to the world what I'd claimed all along, that I might not be the biggest, but I'm the best.

"As for the money, well, I thought about that too. I suppose I should've planned to consult some financial advisers to get set up in the right tax shelters—that's what Howard would have done—but you know what I really wanted to do? I wanted to buy a Farrell's Ice Cream store. They sold for about a quarter-million. I've had the idea for a long time, and I'm always turning it over in my head on surveillance when there's not much action. I like ice cream. But the thing is that everybody is always happy in an ice cream parlor. It's amazing. And Farrell's ice cream is the *crème de la crème*. But they're great merchandisers too. That's what I like. They throw a lot of birthday parties for kids, wheeling out fire engines with the sirens going full blast for all the kids to ride around on with firemen's hats. And the kids are jumpin' all around, yelling and screaming and going wild. It's great. I like kids. The parties are fun for them, and it's good for business. See, Farrell's understands the fundamental principle that kids equal ice cream and ice cream equals kids. Yeah, I can't wait to get my hands on an ice cream store. That would really be the life."

———

Then Lewis went back to the phone.

Just to make sure his information was correct, he put in a call to the Princess desk and asked for Bob in person.

"Just a minute, please," said the hotel operator casually. "I ring him for you." When she came back on the line she was almost breathless. "Bob no here, no here!" she exclaimed. Gil asked her about the other members of the Tabernacle. "All upstair," she said, "all upstair. No talk now." Then she hung up, leaving Lewis feeling very uneasy.

"I was dealing with a high-class hotel," he says, "and it just wasn't normal for an employee to panic on the phone like that. If this was a flophouse in Piscataway, New Jersey, I could understand it, but the Princess? Something scary was happening down there, and I had a bad feeling it had to do with Hughes."

He called Gary Field at the *Enquirer* next to tell him that he'd located the billionaire. "That's great, Gil!" Field replied. "How'd you ever do it?"

"That's none of your business!" Lewis snapped. "Now, look, would you hurry it up with the contract? It sounds like something's happening down there and I'd like to get going. I don't want to lose him." Field explained that the paper's lawyer wouldn't be back from vacation in the Bahamas until the next day, and he'd have to confer with some New York bosses before writing anything up. But he'd work on it.

"Do that," said Lewis.

"I had to play it cagey," Lewis explains, "because I was dealing with cagey people. If I told them where Hughes was, I knew they'd send their own people down there and leave me out of it. I always have to protect my information. But I also knew that there was no way I could convince those assholes that I really had to hurry. They'd just figure I was trying to pressure them. To tell them about trouble ahead would've been like trying to warn the captain of the *Titanic* about icebergs."

Lewis got to work on his plan. "I figured the people around Hughes would kill to protect him. Christ, nobody knew if he was dead or alive for fifteen years. That's service. We're talking about canine devotion here. I mean, those guys were picking up Hughes's dirty Kleenexes!

"And I knew that the *Federales* weren't going to protect me. Ordinarily if I got jammed up, I might be able to buy my way out. But this time I'd be buying against Howard Hughes, so that wasn't going to work. I couldn't even take my gun, because it's a serious offense to be caught taking arms across federal lines, and there are all those metal detectors in airports to check up on you. What I needed was a decent contact down there."

To find one that Thursday, April Fool's Day, Lewis got a copy of the Acapulco Yellow Pages from the telephone company to add to his considerable collection. Searching through under "DETECTIVES," Lewis came across the familiar name of William Clancy, who'd helped him out in the Bahamas a few years back when Lewis was tailing a woman who had left her husband to frolic around the world with an all-star hockey goalie.

Reached by phone, Clancy said he'd be only too happy to provide spare photographic equipment, just as he had in the Bahamas, and also to get hold of various modes of rapid transit: a speedboat, a motorcycle, a bicycle ("a great way to get short distances fast without attracting attention," says Lewis), and a private plane, which Clancy himself owned.

"Say, this doesn't have anything to do with Howard Hughes, does it?" asked Clancy when the detective came to the end of his shopping list.

"Why do you ask?" replied Lewis.

"Well, everybody and his brother is trying to find out if that son-of-a-bitch is down here."

"Isn't that interesting," said Lewis in a so-what voice, pleased that everyone else was still looking.

Then Lewis paid a call on a travel agent downtown. He told the girl that he was planning a trip to Acapulco and wanted to stay at the Princess, since a friend had highly recommended it. "But I do have one special request," Lewis went on. "My wife and I will be traveling with another couple, and they thought it might be fun to stay someplace that had a view of our room at the Princess. You see, we want to be able to wave to each other from the balcony while we eat breakfast."

"The broad looked at me," Lewis recalls, "like I was Diamond Jim." But she thought for a moment and said there was a hotel that she supposed would suit their needs, the Pierre. She'd stayed at both the Pierre and the Princess herself, and she drew a map showing how the two lined up. At Lewis' request she also drew in all the entrances and exits. "The Pierre gave a good catty-corner view for our twenty-four-hour surveillance," Lewis says. Drawing on the $500 *Enquirer* advance, Lewis booked a double room in each hotel. Roger would use the one in the Princess, making it easy for Gil to come and go. And with their rooms face to face, the detectives would be able to keep an eye out for each other during the investigation.

Roger Grove had said that when Hughes was at the Ritz-Carlton, the billionaire had left his room only at three in the morning. If he stayed true to form, Lewis would need more than his usual Instamatic to photograph him. Consulting his photographer Duane Smith, Lewis decided to go with twenty-four-hour videotape surveillance using a Quasar camera, the same kind used in banks, and infrared lenses for available-light photography. "With that stuff," he says, "we could film in a mine shaft."

Gary Field told Lewis that the *Enquirer* had all that gear on hand. "They'd been in this business a while," Lewis marvels. He told Field he'd also need a woman to help operate the equipment. And she had to be sufficiently poised to travel as Lewis' wife, since, as he says, "a single, middle-aged guy sticks out at a resort." The woman would have to double as Roger's wife as well, when he needed one. Field knew just the woman; Lewis could pick her up in Atlanta on the way down.

On Friday, April 2, the plan was all set. Lewis and Grove would fly out to Acapulco by way of Atlanta and take up residence in the Princess and the Pierre. They'd carry in the videotape equipment in their suitcases, since it obviously wouldn't do to march in with it over their shoulders. "Who knows how many Hughes stoolies were lurking in the hotels disguised as chambermaids or bellhops?" he asks.

They'd set the camera up on a tripod by the window, shroud it with curtains, and aim it down at the Princess' front and side entrances. Lewis would watch from his balcony by day while pretending to soak up the sun—and at night as if he were taking the evening air. Roger or the *Enquirer* woman would take over when Lewis could no longer keep his eyes open. But the detective would be particularly watchful around 3 A.M., Hughes's prime time. Otherwise, Grove would be trying to extract news of Hughes from delivery people, airport personnel, and hotel workers. When not covering for Lewis at the camera, the "wife" would stay inside the room to keep out the help's prying eyes and light fingers. Says Lewis, "We didn't want anybody talking about the strange folks in room 803 with eighteen pounds of video equipment hanging out the window."

In case the Hughes crowd got wind of the adventure, Lewis would book a spare cottage in town, once he got there, to use until things cooled off; then he'd go back to the investigation. "If I spotted anything from the balcony," he explains, "a member of the Tabernacle, or Howard himself, I'd check to make sure it was on tape, then pack up and get the fuck out of there." He'd drive the speedboat right out to sea if necessary, or fly off in Clancy's plane, or blow out by motorcycle, or by pedal power. "It's nice to have options," he says. If things got really tight, he'd hand the tapes over to Clancy and have him get them out to the *Enquirer*. The whole show would probably take three weeks, four at the outside, and cost around $100,000.

He couldn't wait to get started. But the weekend went by and the contract *still* hadn't come through. Field told him that "a few details still had to be ironed out." It was his way of saying, Lewis learned later, that projections of six-digit expense money for the escapade had sent the *Enquirer*'s New York powers through the roof. But the detective couldn't bear to wait another day. On Monday, April 5, he resolved to take off first thing in the morning, contract or no.

Lewis remembers right where he was standing when he got the bad news about Howard Hughes. He was in the Zayre's automotive department waiting for his wife's shock absorbers to be replaced. Suddenly his son Danny raced in yelling that he'd heard on the radio that the billionaire was dead.

Lewis just smiled. "A little late for an April Fool's joke, kid," he said. But it was no gag. Hughes had died on a plane from Acapulco to the Texas Medical Center that morning.

"The coincidence on that case," says Lewis, "was really something. I couldn't believe the guy was really dead. I waited so long for a break like that, and then, *after twenty years,* Howard up and croaks on me the very day I'm on my way to find him. You'd almost think he knew I was coming."

That night, Lewis had a mournful conversation with the *Enquirer* editors, who were, if anything, more aggrieved than the detective, although they certainly didn't apologize for holding him up with the contract. Lewis didn't tell them that, as it happened, Hughes was wheeled out the side door of the Princess on the way to the ambulance and the private plane—the exact spot where his video camera would have been aimed. Who knows how much the networks would have given for film of Hughes's last moments? Or how much wire services would have offered for stills? Lewis doesn't want to think about it.

Just to be on the safe side, he dispatched Grove to the funeral in Texas to make sure the corpse really belonged to Hughes. Roger watched the funeral procession through binoculars from a respectful distance. The coffin was closed, but he sidled up to several relatives who assured him that it was indeed the billionaire being lowered into the ground.

Lewis sometimes feels he was buried right along with him. It's usually a cold winter night when the thought arises. The snow is whipping across his Buick, the heater is out, and he has lost all sensation in his feet and fingers as he waits for some giddy divorcée to make a move on a domestic case. Then he thinks: "I'm only here because of Howard Hughes." The thought fills in his mind, and he pictures himself, briefly, on a beach in Acapulco splashing in the warm surf, or soaking up the Mexican sun, before drifting back to the Princess, as the sun falls, for dinner and a long, quiet night in his suite.

Or maybe he's behind the counter at his Farrell's ice cream parlor, scooping sundaes for a roomful of romping kids.

But then, as always, his mind returns to the clients he'd leave behind, and to the secrets locked away in these dark houses lining the snowy street. Then he thinks, "There will be another Howard Hughes." And he sets his eyes once again on a distant window, and hunkers down once more for the long, cold night.

"I tell you, I'm not Miss Marple."

NINE

A Real Mystery

Lewis generally avoids detective novels, but he did once pick up a Robert B. Parker mystery after hearing so much about Parker's Boston-based detective, Spenser. He got through five pages and then threw the book down in disgust. "I got to the part where a client comes to this Spenser to find out who killed his brother," Lewis recalls. "Now, that's just silly! You don't go to an investigator for that. You go to the cops. They're the only ones with the resources to mount that kind of investigation. That guy Parker might have ridden around in a few cop cars or something, but he has *no* idea of reality."

Lewis pauses for another gulp of coffee as he sits by his phones in the living room. Grandma makes a surprise appearance to rub her back up against the detective's shin. "I stay away from that Sam Spade stuff," he says, "but I know some investigators who read it, or see it on TV, and they try to live out the fantasy. One guy had his name legally changed to James Bond. Can you imagine? Another has a license plate THEYE. Now, how's anybody going to do surveillance with plates like that? No wonder so many investigators are strapped for dough.

"I've seen a few detective shows myself, and the way TV detectives go wrong is in their style. They're always *pushing* the situation by taking off on a high-speed car chase or going for their guns.

That's no way to conduct an investigation. The only thing that's good for is getting yourself killed."

TV detectives are a sensitive subject for the investigator, because he is so often asked if his work is "really like the TV shows." In a sense, Lewis' real competition isn't First Security or Pinkerton's so much as it is *Rockford* and *Magnum, P.I.* And he has come to expect his clients' disappointment when he says that in truth, his work isn't quite so glamorous; that he has never shot anyone, rarely even carries a gun, and drives only secondhand cars.

But if, fundamentally, Lewis' character does resemble the hard-boiled p.i. of fiction, in his combination of toughness and sentimentality, irascibility and charm, Lewis himself is loath to admit it. He resents any suggestion that he might have styled himself after the fictional heroes, trying on tough-guy poses in the mirror. "It's just the job," he says. "I have to act tough or I can't operate. If I got into that emotional morass with my clients, I'd never get anything done."

And, making a clean sweep of the foundations of detective fiction, Lewis expresses little interest even in mysteries. He acknowledges that some of his cases have a "puzzle quality"—particularly the missing-persons ones—but he insists that he often has to ignore the darkest, most bewildering elements, or he'd be stuck on one case forever.

"Take the Pinkham case," he says. "There was plenty of mystery to that one. If I were Miss Marple, I'd still be sitting behind a stack of books in the library puzzling over it. But I knew my job wasn't to figure Pinkham out. My job was to find him."

Lewis takes another swallow of coffee, gives Grandma a pat, and launches into the tale.

The Pinkhams' driveway, he remembers, went on for a hundred yards past the stables and a caretaker's cottage before it reached the stone mansion with its slate roof and dozen chimneys. The maid ushered the investigator into the library, where he found the Pinkhams warming themselves with cocktails and a blazing fire. The flames glowed on the gold wallpaper. Ted Pinkham was a tall, barrel-chested gentleman in a brown cardigan; Alice, nearly as tall as her husband and wearing a frilly white blouse with a handkerchief stuffed up one sleeve, reminded Lewis of his first-grade teacher. Ashen-faced, the two seemed to have passed into what the detective calls "low-grade shock."

Three weeks before, Ted Pinkham explained, they'd found a note from their twenty-nine-year-old son, Ned, on the dining-room table. They handed it to Lewis to read. Typed out on Edward F. Pinkham, Jr., letterhead, the letter was strangely formal and said only: "Circumstances dictate that I depart. Thank you for everything you've done."

There had been no sign of Ned since.

"Mr. Lewis," Ted Pinkham concluded, "we're afraid something has happened to our son. We'd like you to find him."

Lewis replied that he'd need more information to work with. Could the Pinkhams think of any reason Ned would want to leave?

That was just it, they said. Everything seemed to be going so well!

The parents described Ned as a tall, skinny version of his father, and explained that he'd been quite successful in the last few years as a consultant to some of the high-technology companies that had sprung up around Boston. He worked out of an extra room upstairs that they'd furnished for him as an office.

He'd "had some problems," they admitted. Ten years before, in 1968, Ned had shocked everyone by refusing to go to college, instead heading west on a motorcycle. The Pinkhams had received occasional postcards from him, but Ned had never given a return address. In 1970, they got a note from Toledo saying he'd married a female disc jockey named Raye Bright. He enclosed a picture— the only one his family had of him. "Ned never liked to be photographed," said Alice Pinkham. She gave Lewis the photo: it showed a frail man in baggy trunks standing by a pool next to a tall blonde in a bikini. The woman, Raye, shines a wide Dolly Parton smile to the camera. Ned just looks sour. The marriage ended in divorce five years later when Raye moved in with someone else. Ned never talked too much about this phase of his life, and his mother suspected that Ned felt overshadowed by his high-salaried, celebrity wife.

The Pinkhams received another postcard from him later that said he'd taken a wilderness survival course and it had changed his life. "I'm a new man," he wrote shortly before returning East to start his work as a high-tech consultant. The transition had seemed painless, and the Pinkhams were happy to have their renegade son back home again.

Now Ned spent most of his days out on business appointments, leaving early in the morning in his suit and carrying a briefcase. He'd come back at six to spend most evenings over his books and papers in his upstairs office. He was so successful that a consulting group in Littleton, New Hampshire, asked him to join the staff on a one-day-a-week basis.

The parents were especially pleased that he'd found a girlfriend, a waitress in a nearby ice cream parlor, although they supposed she was "somewhat beneath him." They were sorry Ned had never brought Jeannette home to meet them. Nevertheless, as a reward for his professional and social success, they'd given him a yellow Audi to wean him away from the motorcycle. But now it looked as if Ned had climbed into the Audi and just driven off.

"I asked them to show me Ned's office and bedroom," Lewis explains, "because I wanted to get a sense of the guy." The office was equipped with the usual typewriter, filing cabinet, telephone, and desk—all of which had been supplied by the parents. Lewis did notice that it didn't have the usual stacks of books and papers that you find in most offices. The mother told him that Ned was "always very neat." Lewis looked through the desk drawers, but found nothing except letterhead stationery, pencils, and paper clips. But the filing cabinet was crammed with hundreds of folders, each one containing annual reports or newspaper clippings about such companies as Raytheon or Digital. Lewis glanced through a bunch of them, then stuck them under his arm to take home. He also found some road maps in the back of the cabinet that he thought might be helpful, so he took those too. He even poked into the wastebasket in hopes that there'd be some crumpled note that might give him a clue where Pinkham had gone, but the basket was empty.

"This guy was so anal I figured if he left anything behind at all, he'd probably try to destroy it," Lewis goes on, with a laugh. "So I asked them if I could check the fireplace. The parents looked at me kinda funny as I went through the ashes with a pair of tongs. But I pulled out quite a few scraps of charred paper. They called in the maid, who came back with a Baggie to carry them away in."

The bedroom was just as neat. The Pinkhams had gone through Ned's bureau and told Lewis the only thing missing was a heavy blue sweater. The ashes in the bedroom fireplace produced nothing, and the wastebasket too was empty.

Back in the library, Lewis tried to reassure the parents by saying it seemed to him that Pinkham had run off just as he had at eighteen. He'd taken care of himself then, hadn't he? "Don't worry, I'll pull him out for you," he said.

The couple seemed to brighten at the idea.

Back in Wollaston, the first thing Lewis did was take out a magnifying glass to examine the charred scraps of paper he'd plucked from the fireplace. "I thought they might have had an address or something he didn't want the parents to know," Lewis explains. Unfortunately, the scraps didn't seem to say anything about where Pinkham might have gone. "They just looked like a row of figures—the normal scratchwork of a business consultant," Lewis guessed.

He also looked over the road maps, but found no markings to give away the route Pinkham had taken.

A little disappointed not to make any quick breakthroughs, Lewis put the papers and maps aside in favor of his usual missing-persons procedure. He settled down in his chair, propped his telephone up on his shoulder, and started calling around for life signs. At this point the Pinkham case began to turn strange.

"I couldn't get anything on the guy!" he recalls. "First I checked with the state police, and found out that the Audi was registered to Pinkham like the parents said, but it hadn't shown up anywhere in state. The police in the surrounding states didn't have anything on the car either. I thought Pinkham might have gotten in touch with his ex-wife, Raye Bright, and after five calls I got her in Chicago. But she hadn't heard anything from him since the breakup.

"I called my friend at the phone company and found out Pinkham had *never* made any long-distance calls from his office phone. Not one. After that, I checked with my contacts at the credit companies for his charge receipts and it turned out Pinkham never even *had* a credit card. That was unusual for a fancy business consultant."

Puzzled, Lewis tried to reach the Littleton consulting group, but a call to the town's chamber of commerce revealed that no such group existed in the area. The detective decided to pay a call on some of Pinkham's client firms. Driving from one sprawling headquarters to the next on Route 128, the ring road around Boston, he talked to people in personnel, asked receptionists, examined records, even spoke to gate attendants. No one, anywhere, had ever heard of Edward F. Pinkham, Jr. Nor did they recognize his picture.

Now Lewis was getting rattled. How could the parents be so wrong about their son? What had he done all day? Did this Pinkham even exist?

Half-expecting another dead end, Lewis swung by the ice cream store to look for Pinkham's girlfriend, Jeannette Hinckley. Lewis glanced around the shop and was relieved to find a waitress with the name Jeannette on her I.D. badge. She was a short, harried young woman, with strands of reddish hair falling down out of a bun. He took a seat at her end of the counter and ordered some ice cream.

When she brought it, he asked, "Say, aren't you Jeannette Hinckley?"

"Yes, that's me," replied the waitress, a little surprised.

"Ned told me about you," the detective went on, spooning casually.

"Ned Pinkham?"

"Yeah, he's an old friend of mine," Lewis explained. "He talks about you a lot."

"Me? Come on. I hardly know the guy. He just stops in here every day after he leaves the library."

"Library?" Lewis repeated, dabbing at the corner of his mouth with a napkin.

"Yeah, the one across the street. He's always got a ton of books when he comes in."

"But what about his consulting work?" asked Lewis, more confused than ever.

"I don't know anything about that. He never mentioned it. He told me he was planning to start a school someplace in New Hampshire. Littleton, I think he said."

Lewis finished his ice cream and hurried across the street.

The library was a big brick building that smelled of floor wax on the inside. "I'm looking for a friend of mine," Lewis explained to the librarian. "A tall guy, about thirty, wearing a business suit."

"I know just whom you mean," replied the librarian. "He used to come in here nearly every day for the last two years—sat in that corner over there in the business section with a mound of books around him all day long. He never even budged."

"Has he been in lately?"

"No, not for a few weeks now."

Looking over the books in the library, Lewis suddenly had an idea about the notations he'd discovered in those scraps from the fireplace and hurried back home to check it out. He spread them all out once again and realized, with a trace of embarrassment, that what he'd taken to be a businessman's computations were really the library call numbers of the Dewey Decimal System.

———

The next morning, Lewis put in a call to the town library to find out just what Pinkham had been reading all these months. "The guy must have read me back about a dozen titles," he says. "A lot of them were books on business, science, or technology, but they all took a weird angle on it—like black magic, secret societies, the occult, or some kind of conspiracy. *A Sense of the Cosmos: The Encounter of Modern Society and Ancient Truth* was one. Another was *Magic, Science and Religion.* And then there was *Contract, Combination, or Conspiracy?*"

A worse shock came when the detective went back to the maps that he'd pulled from the back of Pinkham's filing cabinet. So absorbed had Lewis been in the highway maps, he had completely overlooked a small Geological Survey Map that was tucked in among them. It was smudged and wrinkled from use, and its creases were so worn that Lewis was afraid it would rip apart in his hands.

It was a contour map of the greater Boston area, Lewis could see, but what had Pinkham been using it for? "Pinkham, or somebody, had put a red dot on each of the towns along 128 with high-tech companies," Lewis remembers. "There was a notation: *'Major Lines of Communication.'* And there were markers I remember from the military showing the course of advancing troops. You know—big sweeping arrows that might show the attack route of some North Korean guerrilla outfit. It looked like Pinkham had all those companies linked up in some conspiracy to strangle Boston!

"I'd definitely hit on something big, and at first it spooked me. All the time this guy was supposed to be doing high-powered consulting work, he was living out a secret life in the library trying to prove these big-name companies were in cahoots to take the state capital. I suppose I could have gone back to the library to nail down all the references, maybe looked for notes in the margins that might have given me a better idea about Pinkham. Who knows, maybe there *was* a conspiracy, and I'd have figured it all out if I'd just looked in those books.

"Well, I tell you, I'm not Miss Marple and I don't have time for that. I didn't really care whether Pinkham skipped town because he had paranoid fantasies about World War Three breaking out in Boston, or because his own double life just got to be too much for him. I had to deal with reality. And the reality was that I was hired to find Pinkham. To do that, I had to look for patterns, and the important one had nothing to do with a conspiracy. It had to do with Littleton, New Hampshire. The heavy sweater, the nonexistent consulting firm, the plan to start some school, the feeling I had that Pinkham just wanted to get away from it all. Everything was pointing in that direction. I had the whole day ahead of me, so I took off in my car and headed north."

In Littleton, Lewis stopped in at the two-man police station on Main Street. "I'd left a message with the New Hampshire State Police to call me if an abandoned Audi with Pinkham's registration showed up, but I knew they'd take their time about it. I figured that in New Hampshire, the only thing to do was go straight to the local police station. If the car turned up anywhere around there, they'd be the ones to find it."

The hunch was sound. Sergeant Berwick, at the desk, knew all about the Audi. "We had it towed in here just yesterday," he said. "Why? What's it to you?"

Lewis started to explain, but the sergeant was not impressed to hear about a big-city detective looking for a runaway. Only when Lewis hinted that Pinkham was a bit "unstable" did Berwick agree to show him the car. It was right out back of the station.

Lewis searched the inside for some clues to Pinkham's mood or plans. A set of directions, maybe, or some empty beer bottles, or— Lewis couldn't help thinking by now—the wrappings from a recently purchased handgun. Maybe Pinkham wasn't up here just to practice his survival techniques. But the detective found nothing. The car was just as neat as Pinkham's office back home.

When he asked where the car had turned up, Berwick directed him to a trailhead a few miles out of town. But when Lewis suggested the police join him with a search party, Berwick stopped cooperating. "A couple thousand hikers tramp through there every summer," he said. "If there's a body up on the trail, somebody'll smell it before too long."

"And if he's alive and needs help?" asked Lewis.

"Well, you tell me, Mr. Lewis. You say he's been missing over three weeks. We've had snow and rain since then, and it's still too early to be trapping animals or picking berries up there. I'd say if he's stayed alive this long, he can wait a little longer."

So Lewis found himself tramping up and down the trails alone. "I was carrying my binoculars, so I could look off to either side of the trail, but I was wearing myself out. I'm not much of a hiker. It was early spring, and the birds were hopping around, and the trees were just beginning to bud. It was peaceful, the air smelled fresh, and there weren't many other people on the trails, since it was still so muddy.

"But I knew that three weeks earlier it would have been cold and miserable. If Pinkham had been thinking of killing himself, there wouldn't have been much around here to cheer him up.

"I was sitting down for a little rest when I heard some squirrels jabbering off to my left. They were jumping all around and dashing up into the trees, so I pulled out my binoculars to have a look, and a little patch of blue caught my eye. I climbed down from the trail to get a better view, and I saw him. I knew right away it was Pinkham. It was awful! His body had been all ripped up by rodents. That blue sweater was all in shreds, and they'd chewed at his hands, face, body, everything—leaving open wounds that looked like a hundred little mouths. There was a .25 automatic lying next to him. He'd shot himself in the head and then gone down.

"I couldn't bring myself to roll him over to get out his wallet and check the I.D. I just made a note of exactly where the body was, and got out of there to call the cops.

"I called the family as soon as the cops were sure. I got the father, and told him what had happened. I didn't go into any of the stuff I'd found out about the conspiracy books and the phony consulting business. I figured he had enough troubles. He didn't sob or anything on the phone. Just thanked me for telling him and that was it.

"I never did send a bill on the case. They'd had enough of a loss already."

Lewis was swirling the cold coffee that was left in his mug. "Like I said, mysteries only get you sidetracked. If you get caught up in them, you stop noticing the facts, the evidence, the *real* direction of a case. Now, that can take you from here clear to California, and it often does. But there are no real mysteries in this business. I'm not even sure there are mysteries in life. There's variety; there's perversion and depravity and insanity. But people are really very simple—they do things for reasons. And I can tell you lots about that."

"If a normal, red-blooded American male gets interested in that stuff, maybe I'm not a normal, red-blooded American male."

TEN

Action

The photographs are dark, grainy blowups in eight-by-ten. But the shots are so powerful Lewis keeps them locked up in a safety-deposit box at his bank. "You could destroy somebody with glossies like these," he says. And Lewis almost did.

To get them, Lewis and his photographer Duane Smith burst in on a couple making furtive love in the knotty-pine family room of a suburban ranch house.

In the first photo the two are still hard at it on the vinyl couch. In his eagerness, the man—black-haired, clean-shaven, corporate—hasn't bothered to remove his shirt, tie, or socks. Wedged between the woman's thighs, his body screens hers from the camera—except for two fleshy arms gripping his back, and a pair of chubby legs scissoring his rump.

By the second photograph, the lovers have sensed something awful is happening to them. He's pulled free from her embrace and turned, dazed, to find out what. The woman already knows. She's craned her head around and fixed the camera with a look of horror. Her plucked eyebrows are arched in disbelief, her chin pulled back in shock. The glowing flashbulb is reflected in her eyes.

In the last photograph, she's hanging on to her lover's tie as though it were a subway safety strap. Her eyes are still glued to the camera, but the man has other ideas. His erection drooping, he's pulling away to find his pants. For the first time his face is visible. It's soft and radiant, almost angelic.

Collected as ammunition in a custody fight, the photographs represent a bit more "action" than Lewis normally bargains for. He charged a whopping $5,000 for the service, since lightning strikes like this one for Leonard Jenkins are hard to arrange and even harder to pull off safely. He still wouldn't have tried it if his client's wife, Elise Jenkins, hadn't accused her husband of molesting their eight- and ten-year-old sons. "Leonard swore to me there was nothing to it," Lewis explains. "And I believed him, but an allegation like that is so powerful that I had to come up with something on her that was just as damaging or Leonard would never see his kids again."

And that's what he did—catching Elise writhing underneath the local bank manager in the Jenkins family room. Nothing could have been more effective. As Lewis says, "Everyone suddenly gets reasonable when you've caught them with their legs open."

But the Jenkins candids had been trickier to get than most. For most of his adultery cases, it's enough to snap his subjects strolling arm in arm down the sidewalk, or shooting off to a weekend love nest in their cars—adulterers are careless that way. But when it comes to catching them in the ultimate private act, almost everyone bars the doors, pulls the shades, and drops out of sight.

Because of the privacy statutes, Lewis normally can't do much more than instruct Duane Smith to set his telephoto lens on a chance gap in the curtains, or wait for an open window on a hot summer night. Yet Mrs. Jenkins continued to live—and conduct her affairs—at her husband's house, although Jenkins himself had moved into a singles complex across town. As the owner, Jenkins was legally entitled to entry, and he was free to invite Lewis in with him.

Something of a voyeur, Lewis found out, Jenkins had kept close tabs on his wife's sexual escapades, and a few weeks later, when he was sure some "action" was developing down in the den, he called Lewis and Smith out to catch it.

It was a chilly winter night, Lewis remembers, around 2 A.M., when the three met at the local Dunkin' Donuts to go over their plan. "Leonard was excited about the idea," says Lewis, "and Duane is always thrilled to help out on domestic cases, but I just wanted to get the shots and get out of there."

The three drove out to the house in Lewis' car. Jenkins led them around through the snow to the back and ushered them in through a basement door. They found the basement stairs in the dark and climbed up silently, then crept down the corridor. Jenkins stopped at the second door on the left and listened. Inside, there were rustling sounds and soft moans. At a signal, Jenkins turned the knob and threw the door open. Smith plunged in with Lewis and Jenkins right behind. He spotted the couple half-naked on the couch in the semidark and started firing.

"I saw the flashes," Lewis recalls; "then I heard the screams— 'My God! My God!'—like that, over and over. The guy jumped for his pants and then lunged for us, but I grabbed him and held him off as the others rushed out. Then I got out too and slammed the door behind us. We almost killed ourselves running down the stairs again in the dark, but we were out that cellar door like nothing. Leonard hit some ice outside and twisted an ankle, but we got him back to the car. Then we all shot out of there."

The photos did their work. When Elise Jenkins got word of them from her lawyer, she promptly agreed to settle out of court, reducing her alimony demands by half and dropping the incest charge. Lewis was glad about that. "By the time I get to them, these people are off the deep end making threats and counterthreats. They do it to take out their hurt on the other guy. But the ones who get hurt the most in the end are the kids—and the kids can't get out there and charge their parents with negligence or abuse during a divorce. They're just hanging on for what they can get, and with the parents so busy fighting each other, that's not much."

But it's the parents he has to work for. Their cases come to Lewis through a dozen matrimonial lawyers around town. About the only common denominators among his clients are their desperation and the wherewithal to meet Lewis's $500-a-day fee, plus expenses. While that may introduce the detective to a higher class of customer, it doesn't necessarily make for a more appealing one. Among Lewis' clients have been the wife who wanted to leave her Cub Scout leader husband after finding out he'd molested his en-

tire troop; an evangelist outraged that his wife was involved in a lesbian affair; and the woman who moved out after discovering that her husband had contrived a special surprise for each of his five daughters on their twelfth birthdays: he'd taken their virginity.

But the majority of these marriages have broken up for a much less dramatic reason: another lover. And regardless of the cause, Lewis' task is always the same. Illicit sex is going on somewhere in all these cases, and it's Lewis' job to find the facts behind his client's suspicions, then collect enough evidence of "misconduct" to tip a divorce action in the client's favor.

Lewis has the routine down pretty well by now. It's generally a matter of establishing "inclination and opportunity," legal terms meaning Lewis shadows his client's spouse to see if he or she seems "inclined" toward some third party—as evidenced by hand-holding, hugs, kisses—and if the two have the "opportunity"—long hours together behind closed doors with the lights off—to consummate the attachment. Sometimes he's been out seven nights a week for months on end to catch these strays. "Nighttime," he says, "is play time."

So Lewis has long ago given himself over to a rhythm that's the reverse of his clients'—and of most people's. While they're at play, he's at work. "I have to bust my balls to get enough evidence, because you have to be sure it goes down in court. So you can't just catch the guy with his secretary once. You've got to nail him over and over. You need a pattern, or the judge won't buy it. And the deck is stacked against me from the start, because everybody in court always takes a private investigator who does domestic cases to be a sleazy, 'dese-dems-and-dose' kind of guy, and they're waiting for the opposing lawyer to make mincemeat of me. But I never give them the satisfaction. I make sure I have the information when I go in there, and then I remember: never volunteer anything, answer the questions as briefly as possible, be totally honest, and don't play games." The same law that governs Lewis also works in his behalf.

Although the detective is cast here in the role of avenging angel, Lewis himself knows better than to moralize. "I deal with adultery rationally and objectively," he says. "I know that everybody's fucking somebody. It's human nature. Roger's funny about it. He tends to be puritanical, condemning people for it, maybe because of his Midwestern background. But not me. My clients may come in feeling their case is the crisis of the century, and I do feel compassion for them, but I treat adultery like a general, common occurrence. I tell them, Look, I've seen it happen a thousand times before. The heat goes out of a marriage and people turn elsewhere. I'm divorced. I know how it happens. I can keep my control, so I never cheated on Nancy. I'd never do that. But other people, well . . .

"So I play it straight with my clients. If it's a guy and he's telling me his wife is a pig to go screwing around, I tell him, She's not a pig—she's in love! To a woman, I'll say, That's the nature of man. If they ask me, sort of fearfully, Do you think my husband is sleeping with that woman? I'll say, Of *course* he is. He's over twenty-one, and it's not unusual; it's acceptable. The timing is bad, that's all, because he happens to be married to somebody else at the time. But I tell them they should be glad he is because it helps their custody fight, or their divorce case or whatever. They like the way I look at it. They're worked up at first, but pretty soon they start to calm down and concern themselves more with the legal aspects of the case, and less with their emotions.

"But the thing is, I know my client is probably doing just as much as the spouse I'm following. Sometimes they blurt it all out about the affairs they've had. Their consciences are nagging them and they have this idea that as a private investigator, I'm going to find out anyway. They think I know everything. I'm like a confessor to these people. So I know it's not all one-sided. When you come right down to it, these adultery investigations are all a game for the courts. Adultery doesn't matter to me, but in Massachusetts, at least, it matters to the judge."

From his nightly hiding place, Lewis gets a rare, unmediated view of human nature, more intimate than that of priest, therapist, or cop—seeing people in their passions and furies, loves and hates.

Yet watching day after day, Lewis also sees the drab monotony of many people's lives and, after all this time, he's come to understand their attempts to break the routine, even if it means breaking up a family. "Most guys," he says, "just come home, pat the dog on the head, hug the kids, kiss the wife on the cheek, grab a beer, and flip on the TV, and that's it. That's America. All those guys can think of for variety is to change channels."

So when one of these humdrum family men decides to play some forbidden games, Lewis isn't one to object. Sometimes it actually cheers him up. He still smiles at the memory of the time he was watching the windows of a downtown office building after hours. Suddenly the banker he was pursuing loomed up naked in the window to thump his chest like Tarzan and give out a piercing jungle cry before dropping back down, Lewis assumed, into the waiting arms of his secretary. Another time, sneaking into the motel room one pair of aging lovers had just left, Lewis was startled to find the place a shambles, with mounds of drying soapsuds everywhere—the remains, apparently, of a shaving-cream orgy.

An elderly woman called Lewis once because her husband had upset her by squandering his pension money on a flashy Trans-Am, jacking up its rear, and taking off every night for unknown destinations. "She was afraid the old guy was on the make," says Lewis, chuckling, "but I found out he wasn't after broads—he'd signed on with the Mafia as a nightly numbers runner."

Better still was the story of the newlywed who hired Lewis to pursue her husband when he drove off at night because she believed he was cruising for homosexual pickups. She didn't mind that her husband was gay; she just wanted to make sure he hadn't developed a steady lover. "I followed him a few nights," says the detective. "There was no problem—he was picking up a different guy each time."

Because of the lively nature of the work, Lewis has to put up with a lot of curiosity from clients asking about the "action" on his other cases, or wondering about his motives in their own. "My adultery cases are the hardest part of my business to explain," the detective begins. "Everybody just naturally assumes I'm getting off on the sex. Well, if a normal, red-blooded American male gets interested in that stuff, maybe I'm not a normal, red-blooded American male. If I got excited, I couldn't do the job right. The client is counting on me to handle the case discreetly and sensibly.

"Besides, with the sex, you've got to remember that it's not like seeing a porno movie. There's no story to it, no pace, usually no sound. Sometimes the sex does get elaborate, with all sorts of costumes and kinky behavior, but it's always someone else's fantasy, not my own."

And sometimes, as in the Jenkins case, when Lewis gets too close to it all, the work seems worse than boring or kinky. "Nobody looks good when you catch them in the act," he says. "It's a terrible invasion of their privacy, and when you're right there with them you feel that so strongly you can't even see them as people—it's animalistic. For me it's like looking at a corpse. I look just long enough to be sure it's dead."

——

The money on these cases makes all the difference. That's what the marriage partners are fighting for; and that's what brings Gil Lewis into the fray. The wealthier the client, the more exotic the extramarital liaison, and the higher the retainer for the detective. No roadside motel rooms for affluent adulterers—they go to out-of-the-way resorts. No furtive couplings like the Jenkins affair for them—their taste runs to full-scale burlesque. And Lewis has made several all-expenses-paid trips to faraway places to snag his subjects. He has traveled to Caribbean islands and Southern hot spots, and once sent Grove as far as Copenhagen to do a background check on a spouse's psychiatrist for a custody fight. But the case that stands out most in Lewis' memory is one he calls The Case of the Falcon's Nest.

Lewis first met his client, Josephine Brenner, in the plush, mahogany-paneled waiting room of her lawyer's downtown office. She could have been any one of the wealthy middle-aged women in furs and high heels one sees traipsing through Back Bay art galleries before lunch at their clubs. Lewis sized her up in a moment: well bred, Southern accent, expensive tastes—"You could barely see her for all the jewelry dripping off her"—early forties, and floating on Valium to cope with her depression.

Lewis took her into the quiet back room the law firm reserves for intimate questioning, poured her a cup of coffee, and sat down to hear her story.

She had been married, she said, for nearly twenty years to Alfred

Brenner, a wealthy financier with interests on four continents. Because of his work, Alfred spent a lot of time away from home, and Josephine had always suspected there might be other women in his life. But he'd been so generous to her that she had felt guilty about her doubts. He'd bought her a custom-made Lincoln, acquired Old Masters to hang on her living-room walls, shelled out thousands for Parisian shopping sprees.

Then the year before, for her birthday, Alfred had taken her out to a sumptuous dinner at a splashy restaurant and afterward, driven her to a high-rise apartment building by the river. Expecting a surprise, she didn't question him. Besides, she was too drunk to argue.

He took her up to an apartment, unlocked the door with a key on his chain, and showed his wife inside. The room was dimly lit, and there was a heavily made-up woman dressed only in a negligee on the couch.

"Darling," the woman said to Alfred, "you kept me waiting." She sidled up to Josephine, slipped an arm around her, and purred, "Come on, honey, don't you want to play?"

Josephine slapped her and screamed, "You bastard!" at her husband. Then she ran from the room, took a taxi home, and tried to sleep, wanting to believe it had all been a bad dream. But when Alfred came home at four that morning, smelling of cologne, she stopped pretending. The two fought like cats until dawn, she screaming at him in outrage and shock, he insisting he'd done nothing wrong. He was just giving her a birthday present! Josephine was a prude, he said.

Alfred was home very little after that, and when he was, he kept up a constant stream of abuse—alternately calling her frigid and daring her to go back to his love nest with him. At last, sick of his games, she changed the locks on the apartment to keep him out. She hadn't heard from Alfred since.

That was fine with Josephine—until her bank balance began to run low. That was when she had called her lawyer. He'd managed to get a court order forcing Alfred to cough up $500 a week. But Josephine needed more. And that was where Lewis came in. "I knew what I had to do," he says. "I had to catch Brenner with his pants down."

130

He began immediately. It was simple to locate Brenner's hideaway by the river from Josephine's description, and Brenner's name was even listed inside the front door, for apartment 6E. Lewis also found a closed-circuit TV system in the lobby, a security patrol at every entrance, and a uniformed guard at the gate to the parking garage. "The place was like Fort Knox," he says.

Worse, drifting through the lot, Lewis discovered that Brenner's car, a silver Mercedes, would be even harder to see into than Lewis' own. "It was like a hearse," he says, "with curtains all around. He could drive in with five broads and unless I was right there when they stepped out, I'd never know."

Since the garage elevator rose directly into the apartment building, Lewis wasn't likely to have the chance. The only way to get a fix on Brenner and his guests would be through his apartment windows. But which *were* his windows? To find out, Lewis cruised the parking garage to be sure Brenner's car was gone, worked his old ruse of sneaking indoors behind someone by holding packages in both arms and waving a set of keys to get through the front entrance, then stepped into the elevator. "I pressed the button for the sixth floor and two others," he says, "so that if the guards were watching the lobby elevator lights on the closed-circuit, they wouldn't know which floor I got off on. You've got to be careful in a place like that."

Number 6E turned out to be a private corner apartment on the river side, as Lewis might have guessed. He oriented himself by glancing out the window over the emergency stairs, then took the elevator back down to the rental office in the lobby to secure a copy of the floor plan by pretending he was interested in renting a corner apartment himself.

The next day, Lewis found a good spot for watching Brenner's side windows from the fifth floor of a nearby parking garage. He practically took up residence there for the next few weeks, peering at Brenner's windows from ten to one during the day (in case of a lunch-hour rendezvous), then four to nine at night. He smoked Coronella after Coronella, and ran through several cases of Pepsi trying to stay alert, but the shades were always pulled. "It's waiting for that first break," he says, "that's when you get the jitters and the gray hairs."

It took three weeks, but the break finally came. Lewis was at his post in the garage when a traffic jam formed on the street below, sending up angry shouts and loud horn honking. Suddenly, the shade of 6E went up. A thickset man with a coal-black mustache appeared in the window with a black woman, as thin as he was thick, by his side.

"It was Brenner, all right," says Lewis. "And the lady wasn't Room Service. But the trouble was, they'd only come to the window to check out the noise. I knew I needed something better or I'd be an old man before I got anything through those side windows.

"As I was thinking all this, I just happened to be looking out at the sailboats out on the river, and there was a guy on the far bank watching the action through a pair of binoculars. I hadn't been able to get a look in Brenner's riverside windows because the water was practically lapping at the building. But I wondered—what about that far bank? I got my binoculars and drove around to one of the hotels on the other side of the water and climbed up the emergency stairs to look out the window. It was way too far to see anything with the naked eye, but in the binoculars I could see that all the shades on 6E were up. Even Brenner couldn't resist a river view. I could just make out the guy prancing around in his underwear.

"I knew I'd need pictures, or nobody would believe me. I was a half-mile away! So I called up Duane, and he was all excited, as usual. He told me he could rig up a camera attachment on a telescope to get some shots. The only thing he asked me for was a walkie-talkie. The guy's a C.B. nut, so I let him have it. I rented a suite on the top floor of the hotel and we smuggled the stuff in in our suitcases. It reminded me of my plan for Howard Hughes. Cost eighty bucks a day, but this time I got the dough up front."

After all those hours in the concrete parking garage, this was comfort: room service, TV, wall-to-wall carpeting, double bed, air conditioning, bathroom, armchairs. A detective's dream. There was only one problem: Brenner was in the Bahamas.

Lewis waited eight days in a state of suspended animation. On the ninth day, Brenner was back. At about five-thirty a blond woman in a pin-striped skirt let herself into the apartment carrying an attaché case. Through the telescope, Lewis could make out every stripe. He telephoned Duane. "It looks like action," he said. Duane was on his way.

Soon Lewis' shortwave receiver crackled. "This is Metco Red calling Metco Blue. Come in, Metco Blue," came Duane's voice over the airwaves.

"This is Metco Blue," Lewis responded wearily. "Come in, Duane."

Duane just wanted to tell Lewis he was in the lobby. "Get up here before you blow our cover," Lewis growled. "Over and out."

"Metco Blue," Duane shot back. " 'Over and out' is a military term. You're supposed to say 'Ten-four.' "

"Bye, Duane," said Lewis.

Up in the hotel room, Duane fitted his camera to the telescope and peered through it to Brenner's windows. He was impressed with the view, but told Lewis that it wouldn't be easy taking pictures from this distance. Any heat or mist rising off the water would blur the image. Heavy traffic on the street below would jiggle the tripod. And the reflection off Brenner's west-facing windows would also cause trouble. Gil told Duane to do his best.

Duane brought his eye back down to the telescope. Brenner had come in, and the blonde was fixing dinner while he sat at the table wearing a black robe, embroidered with gold and silver, with a red

133

Oriental seal emblazoned on the back. So proudly did Brenner lord it over the little birds who took such loving care of him in his aerie that Lewis soon dubbed him the Falcon.

As Duane watched through the telescope and Lewis through the binoculars, the woman put Brenner's dinner on the table and slipped into the bedroom. Moments later she returned in a bright yellow halter top and spangled, puffy pantaloons.

"Hey, get a load of that!" drawled Smith. "Whoo-ie! That guy's in for a fun time tonight!"

"Relax, Duane," said Lewis. He was glad his prey was safely out of earshot across the river this time. He remembered all too well the night he had let Smith out of his car to sneak up on a pair of lovers where they'd parked at a crowded roadside hilltop to neck with a view. Suddenly from across the row of cars, he heard some bushes rustle violently and then loud cracking noises. There was a muffled yell, and all the cars flashed on their lights, fired their engines, and shot away. Distracted by the view he'd gotten, Duane had lost his footing and gone over the bank. He reappeared a few minutes later, torn and scuffed. "Where is everybody?" he asked.

Back in the Falcon's nest, the woman put on a record and then, while the big bird calmly ate dinner, danced in front of him, swirling and wiggling her hips like an Arabian belly dancer. Duane clicked madly away at the scene; Lewis just watched, as unmoved as the Falcon himself.

But when Brenner finished his meal, he clapped his hands and the blonde cleared the dishes away. She swirled about him once more and, with a quick motion of her hands, pulled the halter top up over her head to reveal a pair of plump breasts tipped with gold tassels. As she jiggled her shoulders the tassels spun like propellers. Next the pantaloons disappeared and the woman stood before Brenner in only the tassels and a matching gold G-string.

"Oh, *boy!*" Duane exclaimed.

"Just take the pictures," said Lewis.

Soon the rest of the woman's costume was gone as well. She was dancing closer to him now, rubbing each breast up against his cheek. Finally she pushed her hands into his robe, knelt before him, and put her face between his legs. At last Brenner's face relaxed into a thin smile.

134

Duane developed the pictures the next morning, and many of them came out as if he'd been standing right next to the duo. But Lewis knew they wouldn't be enough to convince a judge. Brenner could argue that this was just a one-night fling, nothing serious, a temporary diversion. "I needed more," says the detective.

He kept watch for nearly two months, and Brenner's sexual Scheherazade act continued the whole time. Lewis had Duane photograph everything: the erotic dancing, the costumes (Brenner had a closetful), the kinky sex. Duane enjoyed the blonde particularly. "Whenever I'd call to tell him there was action," Lewis recalls, "he'd ask, 'Is it the blonde?' He'd be there in a flash if it was."

Lewis himself had no preferences. Tailing the women as they left, Lewis found out that Brenner actually flew them in from as far away as Paris and Korea. Others came from New York, Chicago, and Miami. Lewis could see that Brenner's secret sex life had become all-absorbing—no wonder he wanted to get his wife into the act.

In two months, the case was done. Lewis furnished Josephine's lawyer with a sixty-page report citing dates and times of the "action" along with thirty glossy photographs and a bill for a total of $21,000. The lawyer took one look at the evidence and saw that he had a bargain. When he met with Brenner's lawyer later that week, he simply removed the glossies from his briefcase and laid them face down on the opposing lawyer's desk, then flipped them over one by one.

Josephine got all the alimony she asked for.

But now Josephine wanted something else. About a month into the case, she'd asked Lewis if she could see for herself what her husband was up to. Lewis had been keeping her informed of the developments, and calling her every time he ran up another $2,000 on his bill. Surprisingly, Lewis agreed to the idea. Even though Josephine's presence might prove an unnecessary complication, he believes in the therapeutic effect of cold reality after months and years of deception—some wives come to doubt their sanity after they've been lied to for so long. When Josephine joined him in his hotel lookout, he didn't doubt the wisdom of his approach.

"She looked horrible," Lewis remembers. "She'd lost thirty pounds from nervousness and dread over the breakup. Her skin

135

was blotchy and her eyes sunken. And she was hitting the Valium harder than ever. She needed some sort of shock to jolt her into action again."

Brenner entered his apartment shortly after his wife arrived across the water. And, as always, a woman soon appeared to begin the nightly ministrations. As Josephine watched, the sight of Alfred carrying on with another woman seemed to bring her back to life.

"That stinking whore," she hissed. "What's he want *her* for? She's not doing anything to him that I wouldn't do, and haven't done better a thousand times."

She looked over at Lewis. "I'm prettier than she is, aren't I?"

"Sure you are," said Lewis flatly.

Josephine pulled away from the window and went to lie down on the bed while Lewis continued to peer through the telescope. "Gil," she said sweetly, "you've been looking through that thing for weeks. Your neck must ache. Come on, let me massage it."

She patted the bed next to her.

Lewis just looked over at her.

"I'm all right," he said curtly. "If I want anything I'll call Room Service."

"Well," replied Josephine after a pause. "You're pretty professional, aren't you?"

"Damn right."

"I like that in a man," Josephine persisted.

"So do I," said Lewis, and turned back to his telescope.

———

It wasn't the first time Lewis had been propositioned on a domestic case. To many of the betrayed housewives he works for, Lewis is the first man they've felt close to in years. He's listened to their stories as carefully as any priest or therapist, and for many this creates an intimacy they've never experienced with their runaround husbands. Living lives of virtual celibacy in the houses they clean and decorate for these absentee spouses, many women feel stirred to the first sexual feelings they've had in years when they see their husbands are cheating on them. And Lewis is the nearest available man. It's difficult for them to understand that Lewis' concern is only in the line of business, and that his interest in their private lives isn't sexual.

"They don't really care for me personally," he says. "They're looking for a spite-fuck. They're always telling me they don't know what they'd do without me," Lewis notes, "that I've done what attorneys, doctors, and psychiatrists haven't been able to do, that I've saved their life."

To discourage them from expressing their appreciation more tangibly, Lewis has adopted a rigid hands-off policy. He never offers his arm when crossing the street, never touches them reassuringly, *never* pecks them on the cheek.

Even so, one woman entreated him to take out her bill "in trade." Another sent him a five-inch-thick roll of ticker tape with the words *"I love you"* handwritten all the way through. Lewis has filled a drawer with billets-doux from a third. And a fourth mailed in a photograph of herself nude to the waist. "If you want to see the rest of me," she wrote, "you know the number."

He shrugs off such propositions, saying they are an inevitable consequence of his intense involvement in their personal lives.

Lewis, however, is there neither to pull the couple apart nor to put them back together. His role is to set matters straight by presenting his clients with the facts they've paid him to collect. He is dedicated to the idea that seeing is believing, and he sometimes even gives up his blessed solitude to let the cheated-on wives or husbands accompany him at night in his car.

As with Josephine Brenner, Lewis is convinced the sight of the errant spouse in action can snap these strung-out housewives or brokenhearted husbands out of their depression. And many clients may well be better off for it in the long run. But it can be traumatic for his client too, and Lewis watches his passenger carefully. One wife, observing her husband with his mistress, threatened to slice off his genitals and stuff them into his mouth. Another woman was just as furious to be stood up by her husband on her fiftieth birthday. When Lewis called to say her husband had gone parking with a neighbor at a nearby lovers' lane, his client, gleeful at the news, drove out to the spot, pulled her car up next to her husband's, and gently tapped on his window. As the detective watched, the husband timidly rolled the glass down to try to explain. Before he could get a word out, the wife slammed her birthday cake in his face.

Hired by another woman to follow her husband on his nightly wanderings, Lewis reported in from a pay phone that the man was necking with his current flame in his gold Cadillac in a Howard Johnson's parking lot. Within minutes, Lewis saw his client's blue Plymouth roar into the lot, loop wide around the hard-top, and like a bull charging a matador, gore the Caddy broadside.

Curiously, it is the wives who are likely to take revenge this way; husbands are the ones who act hurt. One fellow, shown the motel room where his wife was in bed with another man, rushed right in, shoved the stranger aside, and fell to his knees before his woman. He begged her forgiveness and pleaded with her to take him back. The wife planted a foot on his chest and shoved him away in disgust.

Other men, however, get a thrill out of seeing their wives making love with a stranger. Lewis has more times than he can count heard the breathing of his client grow deep and heavy beside him as the two watched the action through unshaded hotel windows.

One grew so excited that he had to hurry off to a nearby gas-station rest room.

"I sometimes wonder why I bother to show these people anything," the detective admits. "They always bail out on me somehow, pouring on the tears, or leaping out of the car, trying to get in on the action."

But he never gives up. Perhaps he needs to share his lonely vision with someone, to get just one of these sorry spouses to see the world his way. But in the end, while a few clients may learn to face the truth about themselves and their marriages, that's as far as it goes. They never see the larger lessons about the danger of passion and the fickleness of love that Lewis has drawn from years of watching affair after pointless affair played out before him in the night. Instead they lash out. Or they sob. Or they turn their eyes with longing to the detective. Lewis is left alone with his philosophy.

"There's so much heat in these people," he sighs. "So much heat."

"My God, emotion controls these people!"

ELEVEN

The Subject Was Murder

It was a little before midnight in a run-down section of town. Four men had gathered in an apartment for a game of dominoes. The jug wine flowed freely, and for a while there was much back-slapping and laughter. Before long, the stocky six-footer Alejo Perez was on a winning streak and started bragging to the others about his superior gamesmanship. His slender, full-bearded buddy Tito Garcia wasn't happy to see his pile of coins shrink and Alejo's grow. He groused about his crummy luck. Alejo snapped that Tito was just a sore loser.

It was too much for Tito. He jumped up, pulled a hunting knife from his coat, and flipped open its long blade. With one quick motion, he plunged it into Alejo's abdomen and then ripped up, opening his pal from the navel to the ribs. Clumsy now, he plucked his knife out, closing the blade on his hand and lopping off a full inch of his index finger. The other players backed off, and Tito started to wail. Alejo, grabbing his belly, hobbled to the door and out to his car, where he pulled a gun from under the seat. He staggered back to the apartment and cornered Tito in the kitchen trying to stanch the bleeding of his hand with paper towels. Alejo blasted him six times in the chest, killing him instantly.

"That's a typical murder," says Lewis, "and God knows I've seen enough of 'em. I'm a certified public defender, which means the court sometimes pays me to do an investigation for the defense, the same way people who can't pay get a lawyer for nothing. Anyhow, when the defense attorney called me on this case it sounded like a hundred others I'd worked on: It's late at night; a couple of friends get into an argument. It gets out of hand, the gun comes out, and bang! a guy's dead. Murder is a direct, brutal act. It's almost never an Agatha Christie, poison-in-the-brandy-snifter routine. Killers feel—they don't think."

In that frantic moment of uncontrollable rage, people will grab anything—scissors, bricks, jumper cables, baseball bats—to take revenge. "The only common denominator," says Lewis, "is the hair trigger on the killers' emotions. My God, emotion *controls* these people!"

When a plumber found out he'd been cuckolded by his carpenter friend, he assaulted his rival with a monkey wrench. The carpenter struck back with his hammer and cracked the man's skull, killing him instantly. A woman did her lover in at a bar by grabbing the bartender's ice pick and plunging it into her companion's back. Another man, in a fight over a parking space, slit his victim's belly with a letter opener. And a short-order cook, angered by his busboy's back talk, pinned him to the floor and yanked out his tongue with a pair of tongs, leaving him to drown in his own blood.

"But I end up dealing mostly with guns and knives," says the detective, "because they're so deadly. When those come out, you know somebody's going to take the long fall. You don't even need good aim."

In one case, a wife grown frustrated with her husband's scorn of her beloved jazz collection—a symbol, she felt, of their whole failed relationship—forced him at gunpoint to take a lesson in music appreciation. Sitting across from her in the living room, he

endured album after album until at last he lurched out for the gun. A shot rang out and struck him in the knee. The husband gasped once, and then he was dead. The wife couldn't believe it, but an autopsy showed that a fragment of the bullet had hit an artery as it burrowed into his leg, and whisked up into his heart. No more music lessons.

Only twice in Lewis' experience have murderers been so cold-blooded as to plan ahead, hoping to save themselves a trip to the penitentiary. One was a dope dealer who liquidated his partner on a drug run by the Canadian border. The dealer let his victim off at the side of the road to relieve himself in the woods, then crept up with his shotgun to blast him in the back. The killer then whizzed back to Boston at a hundred miles an hour to visit friends and establish an alibi. But Lewis managed to turn up a truck driver who had heard the shot and taken down the dealer's plate number as he sped away.

The other case is still open: the mysterious disappearance five years ago of a North Shore housewife. Hired to track her as a missing person, Lewis hasn't turned up a single life sign. He suspects she was actually murdered by her husband, a pig farmer, who then ground her up and fed her to the hogs. But he can't prove it.

———

Although murders occur in the heat of the moment, Lewis views them with the coolest detachment. Called in by the defendant's attorney after charges have been filed, Lewis doesn't come onto the case until the corpse has been hauled away and the passions have quieted. In fact, he never sees the corpse in a murder investigation, except in the glossy police photographs taken at the scene of the crime, and he has no desire to, either. His interest lies exclusively in the events that led to the killing, the dry facts of the case. "My job is to reconstruct what happened," he says, "just to lay the whole thing out. And the corpse can't tell me anything about that."

If adultery occasionally takes Lewis to the top of the social world, murder always brings him to the depths. Lewis' clients in these murder cases are usually penniless, often black or Hispanic, and sometimes speak so little English that he has to communicate with them through an interpreter.

"Murder is not a crime common to the upper classes. It's the poor who kill," he says. "The rich can take a vacation or run off with the secretary when the tension builds. But the poor are locked into a cold-water tenement someplace and that's all they've got. And murderers aren't usually the most rational people, either. When the anger comes they can't help themselves. They never think to connect their action with any result. I'm the one who has to put it all together for them afterwards. I end up spending a million times more mental energy examining their crime than they did committing it. For them it happens, bang! and then it's over. For me it goes on and on."

Indeed, the amount of time required for these defenses is so high, and the available court funds so low, that Lewis often nets as little as a dollar an hour for his services, barely enough to pay for his Coronellas. "I don't mind. I'm not in it for the money," he says. "So long as I'm paid something, I'm okay. I'm not a do-gooder—I just think these guys are entitled to a fair shake. You can't just give up on them."

Lewis' first move in an investigation is to look at the prosecution's case against his client, obtained by the defense attorney through a "discovery motion." The collection of evidence is often substantial, complete with an array of witness statements, ballistic reports, criminal history, description of the murder weapon, fingerprint analysis, and the medical examiner's results, all of it pointing directly at the accused. "The prosecution tries to make a strong impression to scare the defense lawyer into copping a plea and saving everybody a lot of trouble," says Lewis. "So I always start with their case, then fan out.

"The prosecution has a squad of cops to collect evidence, and the defense has just me, plus I'm working on short money anyway, so I've got to concentrate my efforts where they'll do the most good. A lot of what I do is to keep the prosecution honest. I see if their case is based on all the facts, or just some of them. If it's just some of them, I want to see what they're leaving out.

"But you've got to remember that I'm not there to get my guy off. That's up to the defense attorney. I'm just there to get him the facts—all of them. Some lawyers don't want to know if their guy's guilty because then they can't defend him so effectively. But I don't work that way. I'm going to tell him what's there. If I find a

143

flaw in the prosecution's case, fine. That's good investigation. But if I find some information that puts my guy deeper in the hole—that's good investigation too, and I pass it on to the attorney just the same. I'm there to dig up the truth."

The key source is the suspect himself, and that's where Lewis starts his spadework. Because so few of these clients can afford the stiff bail set for most murders, Lewis generally catches his first look at him in a gray prison uniform at the jailhouse. In Boston, that means the hulking granite Charles Street Jail, a place built in the 1850s and hardly changed since. Lewis presents his credentials to the guard, then passes through a metal detector before being escorted to a big green conference room with one long table and a few folding chairs to meet his client. There, as they talk, the sound of clanging doors in the big stone prison echoes all around them.

"A lot of lawyers are intimidated by their murder clients," he says. "They're often big, physical guys. Even the small ones are dangerous if they're wiry. One of my clients, Eddie, was like that. I was there one day when he tried to strangle his attorney in a courthouse holding room because he was upset with the way the trial was going. I had to pull him off and straighten him out. But that's rare. Murderers may act cocky, thinking they're really tough because they've just killed a guy, but most of them act normal so long as they're separated from the circumstances that set them off. They don't scare me, anyway. I figure I can handle anybody if I can get my hands on them. On a jailhouse visit I'm usually wearing a coat and tie, so I don't look like much, but when I move in close, hunch up a bit, and flex, he gets the message.

"I play it totally straight with the client from the start. I tell him, I want to know everything you know or we're gonna have problems. Then I test his veracity by asking him questions I already know the answers to. Lots of them try to get you to buy some line because they think that's going to help them. But I bore right in on their lies. If all the evidence points to his being there and he swears he wasn't, then I'll tell him straight out that I want the truth: 'You can shit your attorney,' I'll tell him, 'you can shit your mother, and you can shit your priest, but you can't shit me!' I come down on them hard, and it usually has an effect on them.

"And most times we end up getting along fine. They see that I'm in a very unusual category for them. I'm not an attorney, a judge, a

jury member, or a cop. They like that. They know I'm not going to condemn them. I'm just trying to put it all back together."

Yet once a killer gets talking, it's often such a grim picture that emerges, full of violence and gore, that Lewis has to work hard to keep from reacting. "Murderers focus on your eyes," he says, "because that's where they can see your disapproval, with the cold stare. If they get the feeling you're judging them, they clam up. So I keep my eyes steady. I may feel a tightening in my stomach, but I never let it show with a hardening of my glance.

"I might explore around a bit as we're talking to get the whole story, but if I were ever to get all excited and say, Well, *then* whadja do, *then* whadja do? they'd shut right up on me. Actually, it works best if I give the guy the impression that I'm hardly paying attention at all. That way he doesn't start worrying he's telling me too much. And it also makes him get into it more. So the more important the stuff he's telling me, the less interested I act. When he gets to the part about actually putting the knife in, that's the time I look over to the wall and say, 'This isn't such a bad paint job,' or something. Nothing that's going to distract him too much, but just stop him long enough so that he wants to get back to what he was saying and really give it to me. But all the time he's convinced he's not saying anything more than that he likes eggs for breakfast."

And so many clients end up confessing to Lewis. A truck driver, for instance, arrested for the murder of his girlfriend, swore to his lawyer that he hadn't done it. But he told Lewis the truth. He was stirring some creamer into his coffee as he sat next to the investigator during a break in the trial when he turned to Gil, cocked his head, and said, "She sure died hard." Then out came the whole story: how he'd gotten so mad at the way she nagged him about his drinking and the way he slept around that he pulled the car over and smashed a tire iron down on her head, stomped on her with his boots, and left her dying on the roadside. He was "pretty tanked up," he admitted. Lewis passed the information on to the lawyer, who bargained with the prosecution to introduce a guilty plea in exchange for a reduced sentence. "The guy was going to the can anyway," says Lewis. "Things worked out better for him this way."

Lewis finds that the deepest revelations come at the least likely times, often when he is getting up to leave, as though the suspect can't face the prospect of being alone with the truth any longer. Lewis had talked with twenty-year-old Frankie Carson, suspected of the brutal murder of a young woman in a park, for about an hour and a half and gotten nowhere. But as he stood up to go, Carson asked him, "Got a minute for a cigarette?" Lewis said sure and threw a pack of Marlboros down on the table. Carson's hands shook as he pulled a cigarette out of the package—the first and only sign of any emotion. Then he launched into his bloody tale, in the dry, deadpan tone that to Lewis signals a murderer's confession. "As they're talking, I see the brutality of the crime," Lewis says, "but the killers never get into it with any drama. You know they must have been ranting and raving at the time, but they never get worked up when they tell me about it. They give a really flat narrative, and it comes out piecemeal. They don't embellish. If anything, they understate."

Nevertheless, Carson's was quite a story. He explained how he'd picked up his victim, twenty-one-year-old Elaine Bauman, at a bar. She was an attractive girl, Lewis knew from photographs, with sandy hair, a pug nose, dimples, and a nice figure. Since it was a warm night, they'd gone for a stroll along the waterfront and sat down on a bench by the bay. She'd resisted when he tried to kiss her, and Carson couldn't take it. Suddenly furious, he clenched his hands around her neck and started to squeeze.

146

As the tale progressed, Lewis knew it was only going to get more gruesome, but for him now, as it had been for Carson back at the park bench, there was no stopping. Even as murderers pour out the most lurid stories, Lewis has to listen quietly and try to keep his eyes calm.

And gradually the whole story emerged: that when Carson was unable to strangle Elaine, he grabbed her head and smashed it against the bench supports, and when *that* didn't work, he rolled her onto the ground and stamped on her throat. At that point Carson noticed another couple approaching, so he lay down on top of Bauman and covered her face with kisses until they were gone.

He then returned to his task with new vigor. He picked up Elaine by the heels and rammed her down head first onto the pavement, as if to drive her into the ground like a fence post. Finally, when he saw no more signs of life, he walked off and hailed a cab.

With Carson, there was little left for the detective to do except look into his psychiatric history for an insanity defense. But even after a confession, and most particularly after a resolute denial of guilt, Lewis goes on to check out his client's version. "There's more than one truth," he says.

If the defendant can get free on bail, Lewis will ride out with him to the scene of the crime to walk through the incident the way he claims it happened—and then the way the prosecution says it happened. Because the client is the one source the prosecution can't get to, Lewis tries to pull as much out of him as he can. He goes over his story repeatedly, each time listening for a chance remark that might lead him to a new witness or another scrap of evidence that, in turn, might shed new light on the crime.

As his investigation fans out, he attempts to balance the contradictory views given by witnesses and participants of the events leading up to the crime. It's a rule of thumb with Lewis that if two people ever agree perfectly about what happened, they're lying. The murder occurs in a swirl of noise and confusion; the witnesses are frightened and often drunk or stoned; the killer is enraged. "And you're not dealing with the intellectual elite," says Lewis. But even if he were, Lewis believes that when a lethal weapon comes into view, everyone becomes a little stupid. "You're concentrating so hard on the knife or the gun, you're practically hypnotized," he says. "Time slows down, perceptions are distorted. Faces look grotesque, people seem bigger and more dangerous."

Lewis was once called in by the police to investigate two journalists' claims that over in the Combat Zone, Boston's red-light district, they'd seen a cop shove a black man up against the wall, level a gun at his head, and pull the trigger. Lewis spent weeks looking into the matter and located a policeman who had indeed pulled a gun on a black man at that spot to arrest him for burglary. But the officer certainly hadn't shot him. The journalists had imagined that part, their minds outrunning the facts in the terror of the moment.

"Like with the dominoes murder," says Lewis, "I still don't know exactly what happened. I went out there, talked to everybody, and walked through the whole thing, but the accounts never added up. The other two players saw a much bigger knife than the one the cops found. Neither could agree on how many gunshots Alejo fired. They didn't remember where they were standing when the knife went in, or where they were when the shooting started. One of them identified with the dead guy and really pinned it on Alejo, saying he provoked the whole thing. The other identified with Alejo and made him look good, and said he was just acting in self-defense. But my biggest problem was that Alejo refused to offer any defense. For him, it was a macho thing. He wanted to get Tito and he did. And he wanted to go to the can for it, too."

When he's gotten all he can from the defendant, Lewis then turns to the witnesses listed by the prosecution. "You've got to know what the other side is saying," he explains. "Sometimes the cops shade things or leave parts out. I get all of it. You can't necessarily turn a state's witness into a witness for the defense, but you can often get information that will help the lawyer make his cross-examination."

Newspaper accounts may add a few more names of witnesses the police haven't checked—or perhaps have checked, but have preferred not to use. Lewis can often dredge up other witnesses by knocking on doors, or by cruising through the neighborhood on the same night of the week as the killing in search of witnesses whose work might bring them through on a weekly schedule. Lewis is convinced that even the most isolated crime has its witnesses, attributing an almost magnetic power to a raised gun or pulled knife, which invariably attracts attention. And even if there are no eyewitnesses, there are always passersby who might have heard the shots or the screams, or seen a fleeing suspect. "People's heads always turn for drama," he says.

When Lewis is able to interview his witnesses personally, he has to finesse them even more than his clients. Lewis always drives out to meet them at their homes, without calling first. "It goes better if I don't give them a chance to prepare." If they're not in, he returns to his car and waits.

"I've got a bit of an edge going in," he says, "because I'm a private investigator and everybody finds that somewhat intriguing. But I have my ways. I look into their eyes and I call them by their first name a lot. People like that. And I always try to find something I can admire in them. There's always something, even if it's only a nice jacket or a skirt. If I'm talking to a truck driver, I'll say, 'How do you park that goddamn rig of yours? It must be a hundred feet long. I can't even park my car!' Or if it's a fisherman, like I had once, I'll say, 'I'd love to have your life, going out to sea in a boat for weeks at a time. That's really romantic.' And the guy warmed to me. It wasn't an act. I was being sincere. But the big thing is to let them know that I'm not taking sides. All I want to know is the truth.

"I treat these witnesses like they're people I've known for a long time," the detective continues, "as if my seeing them is a reunion. It's important to build up a good relationship that will last you through the end of the case, because you never know how much you're going to have to count on these people. On one murder case, the last person to see the victim alive was a five-year-old named Toby. I must have spent a week with that kid. I showed him my empty gun holster to get him interested, played with his trucks, talked over his Dick-and-Jane reading. He told me all about kindergarten. Of the five or six hours I was there, I probably talked about what he'd seen for fifteen minutes. But like with the murderers, I never let on what he was saying made much difference, even though he was giving me a pretty detailed description of the leading suspect in the case. I didn't want to make him nervous. We became pretty good friends."

As he does with his murder client, Lewis goes over the witness' story several times. "I pull *all* the information out of them," he says. If possible, he takes witnesses back to the scene of the crime so they can point out just where they were standing and re-create what they saw. "I want to reconstruct it from their perspective," he says. "But I check up on them, too. I learned from Mrs. O'Brien in that Wayne Nugent case never to take a witness' sight or hearing for granted. That's the first thing. But I'll make a lighting check, too. I'll even go out to the airport to check on the cloud cover or what the moon was on the night of the incident from the weather guy at the FAA building. And I'll bring back a certified copy in case I need it for court. If the witness was standing in a crowd, I'll want to know how big the crowd was, because it's easy to lose your own point of view if there is a lot of yelling and screaming."

Lewis makes a practice of driving out himself to collect any documents pertaining to the case. "You always have to get them in person," he explains. "Nobody does anything for you by letter or over the phone. Besides, if I'm going to introduce them in court, I have to produce the guy who gave them to me, so I've got to have him on board." These documents may range from a pharmacist's receipts, as in the Nugent case, to employment records that might corroborate a suspect's alibi, to a criminal history for a witness' background check.

Finally, Lewis collects his own experts to go over the technical aspects of the prosecution's case. He consults professionals in ballistics, fingerprint analysis, and forensic medicine to make sure everything tallies. "If the Medical Examiner says he found a .38-caliber slug in the body," Lewis explains, "then I want to make sure the cops have a .38-caliber murder weapon, and not a .32 or a .44, as sometimes happens."

When the whole "package" is assembled, Lewis brings it in to the attorney and they prepare the case for trial.

"You never know which way a jury is going to go," he says. "That's another reason I run so hard on these cases. You never know which little bit of evidence is going to tip the balance."

In the case of Lieutenant Detective Mike Egan, the defense hinged on a single scrap of trash; but then, that was in keeping with the whole smelly affair.

It happened during the gangland wars of the late sixties when

150

rival Mafia families were battling for control of the city. Nearly every week another corpse would turn up in an abandoned car in some lonesome back alley with the telltale two bullets in the back of the head. "The victims were always done in by their friends," Lewis explains. "The Mafia does it that way to make sure their guys don't get their loyalties confused. The killer invites his buddy out for dinner, gets him relaxed and happy with a couple of broads and plenty of liquor, and then takes him for a drive out to some deserted street where he'll plant a gun barrel in the back of his head and pull the trigger."

Lt. Det. Egan was the intelligence officer at police headquarters in charge of keeping track of mob warfare. A sturdy, square-jawed Irishman, Egan pulled his information from Mafia insiders cultivated with small favors. Remarkably, he received advance word on forty-nine out of fifty-two killings at one stretch. For twenty-seven of them he was the first to find the body. One turned up in three suitcases. With another, the face had been peeled away like a banana skin; Egan had to stretch it back over to make the identification.

But now Egan's commanding officers were beginning to think their intelligence man was performing a little too well, and that maybe he was involved in the slayings himself. The commanders had a tip that when mobster Frankie Angelini had been machine-gunned and ditched in a snowbank a few weeks earlier, Egan had promised his informants he'd check on the body an hour after the crime, but hold his report until the gunmen had made their getaway. Egan was arrested as an accomplice after the fact—a murderer.

Facing trial, Egan told Lewis a different story. He hadn't had anything to do with the Angelini murder, he said, and his commanding officers knew it. They were just getting back at him for refusing to give false testimony to bolster their case against another alleged Mafioso they wished to dispatch.

Lewis discovered from his own headquarters informants that the tip had come from a Walpole inmate named Sanderson eager to improve his chances for parole. Lewis also found out that police higher-ups had paid their tipster at least four visits out at the penitentiary to help "organize" his testimony.

But the other witness against Egan was on the outside—a New Hampshire woman who claimed that Egan had bragged about his part in the Angelini murder one night over dinner. Egan admitted he'd taken the lady out, but he'd never mentioned any murder. He had had nothing to do with it! The woman herself was out of reach in protective custody, but the investigator got to her another way—by persuading her former landlord to let him into the house she'd just vacated. "That made it legal for me to go in," Lewis emphasizes, "because I was invited by the owner."

By the time Lewis got there, all the furniture was gone, but the floors were still littered with old papers and trash. The owner had no use for the stuff, and was happy to let Lewis sweep up the place with a broom. Lewis collected a small pile of potentially useful material in crumpled notes, scuffed photographs, and torn envelopes and brought them back to Egan to go over. With a shout, the policeman grabbed one of the papers and held it up to the light. It was an envelope bearing the name of Frank Garner, a convicted murderer Egan remembered distinctly. Egan's testimony had sent Garner away to Walpole in the first place. The man had threatened to machine-gun him in return as soon as he got out.

Now it was clear why the New Hampshire woman was trying to send Egan to prison: Garner had put her up to it, to make good on his threat a little early. And he'd bribed his Walpole neighbor Sanderson to make the first tip, too. Lewis later firmed this up with further evidence from the Walpole visitors' records and testimony from prison guards. Although Lewis never did unearth damaging information about Egan's superiors, he had the goods now to flatten the department's case against the lieutenant detective—and cast the gravest doubt on their motives in bringing it.

The jury wasn't out even half an hour before it returned with a unanimous verdict—not guilty.

——

There is another type of murder suspect, however, who is neither the victim of a single moment's rage, like Alejo Perez, nor the victim of circumstances, like Mike Egan. These are the psychotic killers who commit the most ghoulish of crimes, often against total strangers. "That killing rage is in them all the time," says Lewis, "and it can come out against anyone. That's their insanity." While the police always give murder cases priority, they are especially diligent when it comes to nailing these crazed killers. But Lewis is just as diligent about seeing they get a fair shake. As he says, "If they're going to send the guy away, I want to see he gets sent away right."

The press called Anthony Jackson the "hitchhike murderer"; it appeared that he selected his victims thumbing rides downtown; but the truth was much less clear. The FBI suspected he was responsible, all together, for more than twenty murders, a state record, yet Jackson was tried only for the four with the most striking evidence—among them a twenty-three-year-old strangled in the woods with her bra; an art teacher garrotted in her apartment and then stuffed under her bed; a college sophomore strangled, stabbed, and shot, then nailed into a closet of an abandoned rooming house.

Because of the viciousness of these crimes, the police and prosecution spared no expense in collecting evidence. A task force scoured the city, retrieving Jackson's car from a junkyard to examine it for bloodstains, and even dragging the Charles River to recover a box of several hundred nude photographs, including pictures of many of the murder victims, that Jackson had tossed in.

The defense attorney asked Lewis to help out with the case. Lewis reinterviewed all the police witnesses, summoned his own experts to check the bloodstains and go over the fingerprints on the photo box. He even brought in a botanist to examine the mosses growing where one body was found to see if their growth was sufficiently stunted to account for a body's having lain on them for the sixty-eight days the prosecution claimed.

The evidence against Jackson was pretty conclusive. But Lewis made a breakthrough when, on a pretrial motion to inspect the prosecution's evidence, he secured Jackson's address book, which the police had seized at the time of the defendant's arrest more than three years before. The book listed about a hundred names and phone numbers, and Lewis started dialing all the ones he hadn't tried already. After a slew of disconnected numbers, unhelpful responses, and other dead ends, he finally hit the jackpot when a nurse's aide from a Catholic hospital in New Hampshire spoke fondly of the alleged murderer. Lewis decided to drive up to New Hampshire to pay her a visit. It was worth the trip, for she provided a surprise alibi for Jackson on one of the killings. A rather blowzy woman in her mid-thirties, she confided that at the time Jackson was supposed to be committing mayhem down in Massachusetts, he was actually in bed with her in New Hampshire. She'd brought Jackson home after meeting him at a local discotheque.

To confirm this welcome piece of news, Lewis then consulted the hospital's mother superior, who checked some records and confirmed that the aide had indeed taken that night off. As a courtesy, Lewis didn't tell the nun exactly how the aide had passed it. "I didn't want to get into the nitty-gritty," he says. But he did tell her that as the keeper of the records, she would have to testify to their authenticity in court. "The old lady had seen some TV shows and wasn't comfortable with the idea of taking the witness stand in a murder trial," Lewis recalls. "She worried about what questions they were going to ask. I told her that Jackson's defense attorney would make it easy for her, and that as for the prosecutor, no D.A. in Boston was going to put the screws to a mother superior on cross-examination. They'd sooner grill an orphan."

The nurse's aide's testimony didn't do Jackson much good, however. He was convicted of three murders out of the four and is now serving a life sentence. But he has nothing but admiration for the detective. Last Christmas, he sent Lewis a box of Havana cigars.

———

Generally, when the truth is that the defendant is guilty as charged, Lewis then enters a second phase of defense to find reasons to reduce the sentence.

Many times, the client's instability is so evident that Lewis needs only the briefest conversation before recommending that the attorney go what he calls "the insanity route."

Wilbur McAllister was a hefty lumberjack up for the hatchet murder of his father, Charlie. According to police accounts, Wilbur had been simmering ever since his wife, Sal, had divorced him on charges of brutality. He was chopping wood one day in his father's basement when he said he heard a voice inside his head declare that it was his father who had forced Sal to leave. "Now take revenge!" urged the voice. "Get him with your hatchet!" And Wilbur had obeyed, marching up the cellar stairs like a zombie out of *The Night of the Living Dead.*

Lewis drove out to the house to retrace Wilbur's steps. "The floor was covered with bloodstains and all the wallpaper was spattered," the detective recalls. "I had to pretend it was paint to keep myself from gagging." Lewis followed Charlie and Wilbur's path by the stains—from the blood-soaked chair in the living room where Wilbur had struck his first blow, down the hall to a downstairs bedroom, back through the dining room, up the stairs, and

into a bathroom, the only room in the house that locked. Judging by the way the door was bashed and splintered, Lewis could see that Wilbur had made short work of it before cornering his father in the bathtub and hacking him to pieces.

Lewis met with McAllister himself at his cell in a state mental hospital. He could see that the man had "that cuckoo look"—eyes shifty and out of focus—and his explanation was just as blurry. "Without shifting gears," Lewis recalls, "Wilbur would be telling me about the murder, then he'd jump to an incident that occurred in the mess hall in the service ten years before, then he'd skip to something else. It was total stream-of-consciousness, and he'd readily confess to anything. If I said to him, 'Wilbur, did you hit him a hundred times?' he'd say, 'Yeah, a hundred times anyway.' Then I'd try it later: 'Wilbur, did you hit him once or twice?' 'Oh, I think it was once,' he'd say, 'I don't know, once or twice.'

"I asked him who the voice was and he said, 'the archangel.' Then he said, 'Don't you remember the time at the picnic in Tennessee when Jed showed up and he was telling me about the argument he had with his sister Suzie over the watermelon? You remember that.' I said, 'Sure I remember that.' He said, 'Well, it was just like that.' Crazy as a bedbug that guy."

Lewis believes that all these psychotic killers are pushed on by archangels—or devils—of some sort, and he tries to identify them. As he says, "Once I know my guy is down the chute, I want to know, what made him that way?" Hearing their gruesome stories, Lewis listens for the odd detail that might give their crime some psychological meaning. He was intrigued to discover, for instance, that the murderer Frankie Carson, who brutalized his date down by the waterfront, had hidden his bloodstained clothes under the dust cover of his mother's piano after his taxi ride home. A piano teacher, his mother was sure to find them shortly. Following this matter up, Lewis discovered that when the mother did find the clothes, she said nothing to anyone, just sent them off to the cleaners. When Lewis interviewed her, Mrs. Carson told him she hadn't suspected that anything was seriously wrong. "Frankie does so many strange things," she said. Lewis also discovered that Carson liked to put on his mother's underwear and that the police had once picked him up in town dressed in his mother's clothes and trying to make friends with a couple of teen-age girls. When the mother sent him to a psychiatrist, Carson had retaliated by pawning her jewelry.

"Carson had a psychosis," says Lewis, "that centered on the mother—wearing her clothes, pawning her jewelry, even killing the girl. His relationship with his mother was behind a lot of his craziness. He was emotional dynamite."

One client, for no apparent reason, stabs a subway conductor in the back with a screwdriver. Another bludgeons his girlfriend's former lover to death, binds the corpse hand and foot, gags it with rags, and berates the dead man for a half-hour until the cops come. And a third steals babies from the maternity ward, strangles them, and gnaws them in his kitchen. "Murder's never pretty," says Lewis. "But I can't worry about that. All I care about is the facts. But let me tell you, it does burn me when the judge sends some guy away for nothing, just because nobody is willing to spend the time to see if he's innocent. That really gets to me."

And that's what was happening to Ron Wilson.

"This guy was a victim. He was just as much a victim as the dead kid, Boyle."

TWELVE

Persistence and Patience

It was a bitter cold night in February, and the whole city had turned a dull gray. Ron Wilson, a slim black orderly with a long face and wide eyes, had just gotten off work at the medical center around midnight. After a bite to eat, he had spotted a friend from his neighborhood, James Booker, a large black man, big as a fullback. Booker had offered to drive Wilson home.

The two climbed into Booker's maroon Buick and headed up through Park Square, on the fringe of the Combat Zone. When they stopped for a light, two white men named Cuneo and Boyle, bouncers from a local bar, pulled up beside them in a Mercury Comet, rolled down the window, and started yelling racial epithets at them. When Booker returned the favor, the whites spat at him. Booker spat back. Wilson squirmed in the passenger seat.

The blacks were sober, but the whites were not. Police later estimated that the alcohol level in their blood was .25 percent—a point reached by downing nine whiskies in half an hour.

When the light finally changed to green, the Comet zoomed off. That might have been the end of it, except that when Booker slowed down to take a left at the next intersection, his car stalled out; Booker got out with a set of jumper cables to try to flag down another car to jump start his motor. Cuneo must have seen him in the rearview mirror, for he made a sharp U-turn with tires squealing. And he wasn't coming back to help.

As soon as the two whites pulled up, Boyle jumped out to make a dash for Booker. Wilson, still in Booker's car, did not want trouble, and his first thought was to leap out and run for it, but Cuneo, still in the Comet, froze him with his eyes.

It's impossible to say *exactly* what happened next. Lewis spent weeks trying to reconstruct it and, except for a few key points, never did piece everything together. But what's certain is that a wild, murderous scramble ensued, with whatever weapons were on hand—a bottle, a baseball bat, a piece of a picket fence, the jumper cables, and finally, a knife.

For most of the battle, the two whites got the best of it. "It was all their show," one witness told Lewis later.

Here's what Lewis came up with: Wilson finally shook off the white man's stare and bolted. But Cuneo gunned the Comet after him, driving up onto the sidewalk in an attempt to run him down. Wilson dodged the car and scampered around the corner of a nearby hotel. Then, suddenly afraid for Booker, he turned back and peeked around the edge of the building to see how his buddy was faring. Not well. Boyle had grabbed the jumper cables from Booker's hands. Swinging them over his head like a pair of South American bolas, he backed Booker—armed now with a baseball bat he'd pulled from under his car seat—up toward the entrance of a movie theater.

Wilson ran back to help Booker out, but couldn't get close to Boyle because of the whirling jumper cables.

Suddenly, the cables slipped loose from Boyle's gloved hand to crash harmlessly against a metal grate. Before Boyle could react, Booker closed in. He dropped the bat, pulled a long butcher knife from his coat, and buried the blade in Boyle all the way up to the handle.

Boyle stumbled back a few steps, then straightened and hobbled back to the Comet. He told Cuneo his side hurt, then passed out. Thinking Boyle had been clubbed with the bat, Cuneo reached under his friend's sweater to feel his ribs. When he pulled out his hand, it was covered with blood. Cuneo sped his friend to the hospital.

At the same time a couple of ambulance drivers happened on the scene and, wielding a can of chemical Mace, persuaded Booker to drop the knife. He'd opened a deep gash in his hand during the scuffle, so they hurried him to the hospital too. When the police arrived a few minutes later, Wilson, dazed but unharmed, was the only participant left to explain what had happened. After taking his statement, the cops told him he was free to leave. They'd get in touch with him later.

Wilson retrieved the jumper cables, stopped a passing car, and got the Buick going again. Then he drove home to his wife and two young children, glad to have made it through the night alive.

He was awakened by a call from the police the next morning. Boyle's liver had been sliced in two, they said, and he'd died in the hospital. Could Wilson come down for further questioning? Wilson saw no reason why not.

As soon as he arrived Wilson was charged with first-degree murder, read his Miranda warning, and clapped into the Charles Street Jail with bail set at $150,000.

The police never claimed that Wilson had actually stabbed Boyle. But he was charged with inciting the crime, for Cuneo had told a police detective that Wilson had come at him with a baseball bat. And an eyewitness watching the fight from a nearby parking garage had reported hearing Wilson yell, "Dig him! Dig him! Dig him!" to Booker just before his friend brought the knife out and plunged it into the victim.

——

"The first I heard of the case," Lewis recalls, "was when Rico Shalhoub called me. Rico's a good guy: smart lawyer, maybe a little wild sometimes. He wears cowboy boots and plays the urban cowboy, but we get along, and I work a lot of cases with him. He filled me in about the fight and told me that Wilson was a young kid with a family, twenty-one, no dough, clean. Rico played the youth part up because he knows I'm always sympathetic towards kids. In my book, all kids are innocents, because they don't have the experience to know what can happen when the emotions rise up.

"So I told Rico okay, and got him started on trying to pry some dough out of the judge on the case. That always takes forever. Then I took a trip down to the can to get a look at my client.

"He was sitting in the conference room down there at Charles Street, a dirty, dull place with grime on the windows and hardly any light. I don't make snap judgments, but I could tell right away that this kid was a victim—just as much a victim as the dead kid, Boyle. Wilson was really meek and mild—the kind of guy who'd walk around an ant on the sidewalk. He spoke in low tones and seemed really confused to find himself in jail charged with murder in the first degree. He kept telling me, 'Murder one, man—whew, that's the big one.'

"A pro will give a smooth, articulate presentation of the facts as he sees them. Wilson didn't know what to say. He didn't understand any of it. A total amateur. He kept telling me, 'I can't believe it, man. I was goin' home. I caught a ride, and now I'm here in jail. I didn't hit anybody, didn't cut anybody. What am I doing here charged with murder?'

"Wilson never yelled prejudice, although he may have been thinking it. But I was there so prejudice wouldn't be a factor. I believe that everyone deserves to be tried on the facts—not on their race, not on their background. I was going to bring those facts out. On a case like this, they don't come so easy. When your guy is a poor black, nobody rushes forward to help out. You have to pull your witnesses out and hold them up.

"Wilson was such an amateur he believed that if he just told the cops his side of it, they'd get him off. I had to straighten him out about that. The cops don't want to help you out when you're charged with murder. They aren't going to go out and search for the evidence and the witnesses that will free you. They want to clear the case, even if it means sending an innocent guy to the slammer. I knew the police detective on the case, Detective Bartley. He's a typical homicide cop, a decent guy doing a decent job. But he's buried with work! Bartley goes out only to get leads to solidify the D.A.'s case. Nothing else interests him.

"Me, I was working on short time and short money, so I had to work the case backwards, starting at the point where the knife went in. With a case as complicated as this one, with all the skirmishing and running around, I could have spent my career on it if I'd tried to do much more. Everybody agreed that Booker stuck the knife in. I needed to find out if Wilson knew about the knife. And if he did, did he encourage Booker to stick it in. So I went over that with the kid right away, and he told me he never even saw the knife at all until Boyle went down."

After looking over the prosecution's evidence, Lewis could see that the whole case rested on the testimony of the parking-garage attendant, a young man named Michael DeYoung, who said he'd seen the fight from the garage's second tier. He was the one who swore he had heard Wilson yell, "Dig him!" just before the knife went in. As Lewis read over DeYoung's testimony he took a dislike to the man, and not just because he was nailing Lewis' client to the wall. "There seemed to be something lacking in his objectivity," Lewis says. "This guy wasn't much of a fan of blacks."

To check out his suspicions about DeYoung, Lewis drove out to his Jamaica Plain address, pressed the doorbell, and asked to see "Mike." (He was careful to use DeYoung's first name to imply familiarity.) The young man's father answered the door, and he told Lewis his son was out. When Lewis explained why he was there, the father guessed that Mike wouldn't try to get in touch.

"It might save him getting subpoenaed," said Lewis, handing him his Lewis Detective Agency card. The father replied that Mike wasn't too respectful of authority and he doubted the threat of a subpoena would carry much weight with him. (It was largely an empty threat anyway, since the detective has no subpoena power. He'd have to get that from the judge through the attorney Shalhoub, a tedious and uncertain process.) Lewis said he'd be back.

"I couldn't grab DeYoung at the garage," says Lewis, "because he'd quit the job. So I chased him and chased him. I must have gone out to that house a dozen times, but all I got was the father. Finally, I picked up a plate number off a car in the driveway and traced it back to a girl in the city. I staked out her place one night and nabbed Mike on his way in. That surprised him, but he told me the cops had instructed him not to talk about the case to anybody and then he shut the door on me. So I struck out there."

Nevertheless, Lewis returned to the garage late one night after it had closed to retrace the steps that DeYoung swore he had taken the night of the murder. Lewis discovered that the glare from a streetlight would have disturbed his view of the actual stabbing down below, and contrary to DeYoung's testimony, a side building would have blocked any sight of the earlier fight up the street.

The more Lewis thought about it, the more unlikely it seemed that DeYoung had heard Wilson say anything like "Dig him." In all his years on the street, Lewis had never heard that one. "Cut," "stick," "plug" he'd heard, but not "dig." And besides, with any number of people on the scene and DeYoung at least twenty-five feet away, how could he be so sure he had heard *Wilson* yelling?

What was more, Lewis wondered if DeYoung would have been able to differentiate sounds at all once the knife came into view. "When something that horrifying appears," says Lewis, "your whole body shuts down. You wouldn't be able to hear anything with any accuracy at all."

All this was enough to jar DeYoung's credibility, but to get Wilson off the hook, he'd need witnesses of his own. The participants weren't much help there. All Cuneo would tell him was that Wilson had come at him with a bat, and Booker, in his desperation, tried to pin the stabbing on his pal too. "Ronnie stuck the knife in," he said, "not me."

In his search for the truth, Lewis would need to get witnesses the police hadn't reached, because, as Lewis says, "Once you've given a sworn statement to the cops, it's nothing but trouble to try and change it." And none of the police witnesses were quoted as saying anything nice about Wilson.

Since the incident had occurred on a Friday night at about one, Lewis returned to the scene on Friday nights between twelve and two for six weeks in a row to use his old trick for finding someone who might have happened to see the fight. "I looked for delivery people, bus drivers, waitresses, and cabbies," he says. "They're all creatures of habit." He ran the license-plate numbers on private cars he spotted more than once and called up the owners. He talked to prostitutes in the area, even to their clients. "The hookers were happy to talk to me," he says, "because they're underdogs just like Wilson. And their johns were pretty open once they found out I wasn't a cop." He spent weeks in Park Square and spoke to thirty people all together, but only one had seen the fight, the owner of a local sub shop who said he had been too plastered at the time to remember anything about it.

———

"It was strange going back to Park Square again after all those years," says Lewis, "and walking around my old haunts from my days at Greyhound. I saw the same faces on the bums sleeping at the bus terminal and around the Square. I reminisced a little, too. I went back to Sullivan and Brown's, a bar they kicked me out of after I got into a couple of fights there as a kid. Nothing serious, though. I had a beer and talked to a barmaid who still remembered me. That was nice. I had spaghetti at Mario's just like I used to every payday back when I was stuffing bags. And I even had a vanilla frappe at the White Tower. That was always a favorite of mine. I used to drop in there at two A.M. every morning when I got off work; then I'd catch the last subway home.

"Going back to the same places, I had a chance to think about all the ground I traveled since I left. I've come a long way, I guess. I wondered whether I'd met the goals I'd set for myself.

"It's a lonely job, detective work," Lewis continues. "You've got to operate alone because you've got to appear vulnerable or you intimidate people. And you can't usually tell anybody too much about what you do. You've got to be available twenty-four hours a day. When the phone rings, you can't tell someone you're busy and to call back later, or they might never call back. The client always has to come first. You never know when the next case is going to come in, or how much it's going to pay, or even if there *is* going to be another one. You're not on a payroll. It does mean you don't have to kiss ass, but it can give you the sleepless nights. I've been broke and I've been almost wealthy. There's pressure either way. You've got to structure yourself, and if you don't do it right, you fail.

"But you give the clients their money's worth, plus a little bit, and case by case, you build up a reputation. That's the satisfaction of the detective's life—building a reputation and seeing it grow, just by doing the job.

"I suppose the Wilson case sums up my career. It had all the elements—finding people, the reconstruction, working with the client, digging out the facts. I always give up a bit of myself in all my cases, putting in something that I'll never get back. That was certainly true with Wilson.

"What a hard fucking case that was! There I was, a middle-aged, middle-class white guy talking to all those black pimps and prostitutes. That's the job in a nutshell. Plus it was the coldest goddamn winter I can remember. I was freezing my ass off! That was a couple of years after the Howard Hughes case, and I kept thinking about the beach in Acapulco. I knew that was a little extravagant, but I did start thinking seriously about San Diego. My marriage was breaking up, and my kids were grown, so I thought I might shift out there and start a new agency fresh. I figured I'd gone as far as I could in Wollaston, and I wanted to leave the ghosts in my past behind. Roger could handle things here. I was planning to leave the agency to him.

"San Diego is great. I'd been out there on a couple of cases. The mean temperature is seventy-two degrees with practically no humidity. Seems like the winters here get colder every year, and the summers get hotter. Since San Diego's on the ocean, there's always a steady breeze. I've always loved the wind.

"So that's what I was going to do. I was going to finish up the Wilson case and head west. At this point I was about a month into it and it was getting me down. I wasn't coming up with the proof. I was starting to feel that if Wilson was convicted, *I* was the one who was going to have to do the time."

———

By now, however, Rico Shalhoub had managed to get Wilson's bail reduced to $25,000, a figure Wilson's father was able to meet by mortgaging his hardware store. "I was glad to get the guy back out on the street," says Lewis. "It was good for him, and it really helped the case. I spent a lot of time with him, and all he could talk about was the murder charge. He saw it as his whole life, and that's what it was. It was his life, his family's life, his kids' lives. If he was ever convicted of first-degree murder, his show was *over*."

Together with Rico Shalhoub, Lewis had the three of them reenact the stabbing just as Wilson saw it. The client had been six feet off to Booker's left and a little behind him when he stuck the knife in. From the angle, Wilson wouldn't have been able to see the knife, just as he claimed.

Afterward, Lewis drove Wilson around the little park in Park Square a dozen times, pressing Wilson to remember everything that happened that night, *everything,* as they circled in his car. Eventually, even Wilson tired of it. "I told you already," he'd say as Lewis badgered him to go through it all one more time.

But sure enough, there was one thing that Wilson hadn't told the detective, and it looked like the break Lewis had been waiting for. After the fight, Wilson said, a tall black transvestite named Deke had stepped up to help Wilson get the car started. Ron remembered that Deke was at least six feet four and was wearing a woman's fur coat and high heels. The idea seemed to embarrass the shy Wilson, thereby explaining why he hadn't mentioned such key information before. When the car got going, Wilson had offered him a lift home and Deke had accepted. He lived in a nearby housing project. On the way, Wilson now remembered, Deke had told him he had seen the whole fight. Wilson had even gone into Deke's place for a quick cup of coffee. He was sure he could find it again.

The Fidelis Way housing project was flanked by a couple of hospitals out Commonwealth Avenue. There's no mistaking it for its neighbors, however, what with all the boarded windows, the graffiti scrawled on the walls, and the battered doors hanging loose off their hinges. "These places are festering with resentment and hatred against the establishment," says Lewis. "And that's you if you're middle-class and white. If you get mugged in the hallway, nobody's going to help you." With Wilson along, happily, Lewis wouldn't look quite so establishment. But he brought his Remington along for the trip, just in case.

Wilson guided him to a condemned section of the project where Deke squatted with other freeloaders. A rat scurried down the hall as the two stepped inside the front door, and cockroaches hung in clusters on the glazed masonry. The window frames had been ripped out for fuel, letting the cold air of late winter sweep through. Knowing better than to take the elevator, Lewis headed for the stairs, with Wilson close behind.

On the third landing, he pounded on the door to his left. He could hear voices inside, but no one answered his knock. Lewis pounded louder.

"I know someone is in there," he shouted, "and I need your cooperation if you don't want your friend here to take a bum rap on a murder case."

Finally Lewis heard the sounds of several bolts sliding open and a chain being released. The door opened a few inches, enough for Lewis to make out the vacant gaze of a black man. Behind him he saw an inverted trash can that was being used for a table and a bookcase laid flat for a chair. Smoke from a crude wood stove billowed out into the hall.

"I'm looking for Deke," said Lewis, pulling Wilson around next to him so the man could see his black face.

"Deke ain't here." The man started to close the door again, but Lewis blocked it with his arm.

"It's important!" the detective shouted. "This guy's up for murder one and Deke's the only guy that can help him. When's he back?"

"He ain't going to be back. He O.D.'ed last week. He's *gone,* brother. Dead."

He shut the door in Lewis' face.

———

That was a blow, but Lewis was undaunted. "Persistence and patience," he says—"that's what it takes. It's like selling magazines door to door—it's not the guy with the best spiel who sells the most, it's the guy who pounds on the most doors."

Back in his Wollaston living room, he pulled out the Wilson file to go through the well-thumbed police reports and grand-jury testimony once more. And this time something struck him. Why was it that Detective Bartley's interview with DeYoung ran seven pages, omitting nothing, but that the one with another police witness, Laura Mitchel, hardly went four? DeYoung hadn't had nearly as good a view as Mitchel. According to her testimony, she had been no more than fifteen feet away, while DeYoung was twenty feet up in the parking garage and maybe twenty feet off to the side.

Yet Mitchel, identified in the testimony as a black prostitute, had never been drawn out by Bartley, and before the grand jury, the district attorney had hardly gotten her up on the stand before he excused her.

Lewis revved up the car again and headed out to Mitchel's Back Bay apartment. An attractive woman who identified herself as Mitchel's roommate came to the door and directed him to a neighborhood used-clothing store called Marcel's. Laura worked there part time as a saleswoman.

Lewis found the place. It was jammed with young kids in organdy blouses, floppy hats, and leather bell-bottoms, all of them moving to a thumping disco beat.

The cashier pointed out Mitchel for him: a gorgeous black woman with high cheekbones, thick red lipstick, and a carefree manner. The disco madness, unfortunately, made conversation impossible, but Lewis managed to communicate the urgency of his business and hand her his card. "I could see fear in her eyes when she saw I was an investigator," says Lewis. But there must have been something in his manner that reassured her, because she shouted in his ear to meet her at her apartment that evening at six.

When he buzzed at Mitchel's door again, the same roommate answered, this time attired in a short, tight-fitting dress. Her name was Sheila Waters, and she was evidently conscious of her allure. Twenty-by-twenty-four-inch glossy portraits of Sheila full face, profile, standing, and sitting adorned the walls. There were only cushions on the floor—no couch or chairs. Laura Mitchel sat demurely on one of them, her legs pulled tightly together by a long slim skirt. Lewis plopped himself down and tried to get comfortable. From that angle, as Sheila bent over in her short skirt to pick a magazine off the floor, he couldn't help catching a peek at her frilly blue panties. And he was startled to discover within them the unexpected bulge of a man's genitals.

"Sure it was a surprise," says Lewis now. "Sheila was a great-looking broad. But I wasn't shocked. Why should I care if Sheila was a tranvestite? What difference did it make? I believe in living and letting live. All it did was put it together for me about Laura. To clear the air, I asked Laura if she was a transvestite too. She just smiled and said no, she had had the operation and now she was a transsexual. She was really calm about it. And she was still a hooker, so she was vulnerable. That must have been the fear I saw in her eyes back at the shop."

Mitchel explained that the cops wouldn't have come to interview her about the stabbing if she hadn't screamed at them about the case after they'd picked her up a few days later for soliciting. "I asked them why they were bothering me," she told Lewis, "when they could be doing something really worthwhile like protecting those two black kids I'd seen getting their asses whipped by a white guy in Park Square."

Detective Bartley, she continued, had appeared on her doorstep shortly afterward.

In the last year Laura had been mugged three times and raped twice—once by a policeman. The night before the Wilson affair she had nearly gotten killed by a man who jumped off the top level of the parking garage to kill himself. The body landed indelicately at her feet. So by the time Bartley showed, she told Lewis, she was "ready to lash out."

169

But the strange part, Mitchel went on, was that even though she'd been standing right there at the stabbing, Detective Bartley seemed uninterested in her account of it. That, of course, made Lewis all the more attentive. Yet just as Laura was about to tell him what she'd seen, he gently changed the subject and asked her about the pictures on the wall, and then brought up what Lewis calls "the sexual thing."

"I was sure," he explains, "that Laura had made her mind up not to give me everything unless she liked my reaction. So I didn't want to get into the important stuff until I felt she trusted me. I wanted her to think that I'd gotten so interested in her that I'd forgotten what I'd come for.

"And in a way I had. I mean, here was this gorgeous broad, and yet she was actually a guy, right? But that's the way I always go with these interviews. I'm really interested to know how people become who they are. Maybe it's because I sense that so many people are interested in me just because of what I do, rather than who I am.

"Laura didn't seem offended. She told me that after the way most people treated her, my honesty came as a relief."

She explained that she'd never been too comfortable as *Larry* Mitchel. Tracing it back, she said she'd had a twin sister who'd died in infancy and maybe that had something to do with it. But all she knew was that no matter how hard she tried to swagger manfully on the sidewalk or talk tough, she was sure her female nature showed through. From her early teens she'd supported herself as a male prostitute for homosexuals. Then she'd started dressing up in women's clothes in her room. Eventually she couldn't contain her femininity and walked about as a woman in certain parts of town where she wouldn't be recognized. She had finally gone through the sex-change operation two years before.

"I thought that when I became a woman all my problems would be over," she told Lewis, "but now I know they're just beginning." If before she had felt she couldn't conceal her femininity, now she felt everyone could see she had been male. She hadn't legally changed her name from Lawrence to Laura, even though it was an ordeal being without proper I.D. And she hadn't told her white boyfriend's family, whom she saw frequently, about herself. She figured it was hard enough for them to accept a black, let alone a black transsexual.

"We talked that over for quite a while," Lewis recalls, "and I could sense her warming up. I gave her some advice about the importance of getting established, but nothing heavy. I could tell from the way she was starting to lean in towards me there on the cushions that she trusted me. So when I knew I had her, I cut the conversation back to what she saw."

Though Laura had been talking to someone else when the fight began, she'd seen the all-important ending. She'd been standing by the curb in front of the parking garage only fifteen feet from the point of the stabbing. From there she could see both Booker and Wilson clearly, and she swore that Wilson couldn't have seen the knife from where he stood and that he hadn't yelled anything. All she heard was the other white man, Cuneo, in the car, screaming to his buddy, Boyle, "Get him! Get him! Get him!"

So that was it, Lewis thought. Wilson hadn't incited the crime. He had only been trying to help, just as he claimed.

Lewis would return to the scene of the stabbing later to pace this out and confirm it. There in Mitchel's apartment he had a more urgent problem: how to persuade Mitchel to testify.

"As I said before," Lewis repeats, "so often I've got to pull my witnesses out and hold them up. I laid it out straight for Laura." He explained that if the police felt their case was threatened by her testimony they might go so far as to arrest her for prostitution right there in the courtroom. Certainly they could make her life miserable if she wanted to continue her career on the street. And during cross-examination, the District Attorney would probably try to embarrass her about her transsexuality. But, Lewis concluded, while those were all serious problems, there was a twenty-one-year-old black kid in even deeper trouble.

Mitchel hesitated a moment, and then said she'd do what she had to do: testify.

———

In the granite courthouse, District Attorney Raymond McCarthy presented his case first. Wilson's pal Booker had pleaded guilty to second-degree murder, leaving Wilson to face the hostile D.A. alone. An ex-seminarian who'd made his name

171

stamping out the juice bars that brought minors into the Combat Zone, McCarthy called the Medical Examiner to the stand for the usual recitation of the medical facts, presented a few hours more of expert testimony, and culminated his case days later with his star witness, the garage attendant DeYoung. When DeYoung got to the part about Wilson's yelling, "Dig him! Dig him! Dig him!" McCarthy paused a moment to gaze meaningfully at the jury.

Then Shalhoub, with Lewis sitting beside him, began his defense. Laura Mitchel, on whom the attorney was pinning all his hopes, took the stand last. A little nervous at first, she repeated under Shalhoub's questioning what she'd told Lewis at her apartment: there had been no "Dig him"; Wilson couldn't even have seen the knife; all she'd heard was Cuneo yelling, "Get him!"

McCarthy wheeled into action on the cross-examination. He needled her about inconsistencies in her version of the time of the incident. Then, swelling with rhetoric, he launched a broader attack.

"Isn't it true that you are a prostitute," he began, "or, as they say on the street, a 'hooker'?"

"I've turned a few tricks in my time," Laura admitted.

"Well, then," continued the prosecutor, "isn't it true that you were in fact soliciting, or 'turning a trick,' at the time of the fight?"

"No, man, you've got it wrong," replied Laura. "I just talked to a john. I wasn't asking for anything."

The D.A. played his last card. "You are Laura Mitchel, aren't you?" he asked.

Lewis has warned her about this, but the question still seemed to knock the wind out of her. "That's right," she replied weakly.

"But aren't you also *Lawrence* Mitchel?" asked McCarthy, looking her straight in the eye. Startled by the question, the twelve jury members craned their necks to get a better look at the witness. The courtroom stirred and a babble of voices arose. The judge had to pound the gavel for quiet.

"Well, yes," Laura replied almost inaudibly. The judge told her to speak up. *"Yes,"* Laura repeated as loudly as she could.

"Well, now," said the D.A., "which is it?"

Laura Mitchel paused, looked over to the detective once for reassurance, and then said evenly, "I was born Lawrence Mitchel but I've had an operation and now I'm Laura Mitchel. But," she continued, "I don't see what my sex has to do with anything. If you don't believe me, I'll take a lie-detector test!"

The defense rested.

———

When the jury filed back into the courtroom to deliver the verdict, Wilson stood in the prisoner's dock and steeled himself for the worst. So it took a moment to understand what the clerk was saying: Not guilty.

Wilson broke into a wide smile and then disappeared in a swarm of jubilant relatives and friends. Seeing that Wilson was so preoccupied, Lewis patted Shalhoub on the back for a job well done and then slipped quietly out of the courtroom. "It was a family moment for Wilson," he says. "I didn't want to intrude."

Lewis took a moment to thank Laura Mitchel for coming through so well as a witness. To his surprise, she thanked him even more warmly. She said after talking to him, she'd decided to get her name changed legally to Laura and, after all this time, obtain some proper I.D. "I figured," she said, "since I was in the courthouse anyway, why not?"

Lewis kept on down the corridor and was just about to the door when he heard a voice shouting for him to stop. It was Wilson.

"I was looking all over for you," he said, hurrying up to Lewis. "I just wanted to thank you, man, for everything you did for me. You're really amazing, you know that? If it wasn't for you, I'd be headed for Walpole, just like Jimmy Booker." His eyes started to well up. "I really owe you a lot, and I know I'll never be able to repay you."

"That's okay, kid," Lewis said, reaching out to him. "I'm happy for you. I'm glad it worked out."

Their eyes met for a moment; then Wilson returned to his family. Lewis headed on for his car. The darkness was just starting to fall, and the lights inside the surrounding buildings were coming on. In the car he pulled a Coronella from the glove compartment, lit up, and took a drag. Then he turned the switch and headed home to move on to his next case.

"Sure, the job has its frustrations," he says, "but it's got its rewards, too. If I'd been Governor I couldn't have done as much for that one kid. I pulled him out! I've thought about other jobs. I've considered starting a Farrell's, and I've thought about moving out to San Diego. But I know I'll never do either one. Why should I start over? I'm just like my cat, Grandma. She's out of the house most of the time prowling around, but she could never leave the old neighborhood. It'd kill her! No, me and Grandma, we're in this for keeps."